P9-DFH-421

tofu

THE ESSENTIAL KITCHEN

tofu

BRIGID TRELOAR

PERIPLUS

c o n t e n t s

How to cut tofu • Making a chrysanthemum flower • How to remove excess moisture
• How to change soft tofu into firm • How to prepare tofu for cooking

t o f u

introduction

You probably know that tofu is good for you, but rarely—or never—eat it. Many people in Western countries, if they know of tofu at all, think of it as a "health food," which they think means that it can't taste good. Little do they know that this culinary chameleon can take on all their favorite flavors—and more. This book is for them—an introduction to the many delicious ways to cook with this versatile and highly nutritious food and how to create them in their own kitchens—but it's also for the dedicated who already love tofu. So, embark on a journey of discovery. Be tempted by this nutritional wonder and enjoy its endless

ability to transform itself into, as the Chinese say, "the taste of a hundred things."

What is tofu? Tofu is bean curd, that wobbly white stuff made from soybeans, and is prepared by a process similar to cheese or yogurt making. By itself, the taste is relatively bland, but diced, sliced, pureed, scrambled, grilled or deep-fried, tofu adapts easily to any dish, absorbing sweet or savory flavors from its marinade or the foods it is cooked with. High in protein, rich in minerals and vitamins, low in calories and saturated fats and with no cholesterol, tofu is an important addition to any diet.

It is important to note that the health benefits of the soybean and its natural by-products—such as tofu—are undisputed. It is preferable to eat organic tofu, made from soybeans that have not been genetically modified.

First made in China more than 2,000 years ago, tofu arrived in Japan about 1,000 years later, probably brought by Buddhist monks and priests. In Japan it became softer, whiter and more delicate in flavor than the Chinese version. Relatively inexpensive and easily digestible, tofu has been a staple source of highly usable protein in many East Asian countries in much the same way that meat and dairy products have in the West. It has also been an important part of the Buddhist vegetarian diet.

Ways to eat tofu

Contrary to popular belief, tofu does not have to be bland and tasteless. When its own mildly nutty flavor is combined with other ingredients, it is transformed—with diverse and delicious results. Limited only by a cook's imagination, tofu can be used in enticing dishes as diverse as pâtés, soups, sauces, crepes, strudels, curries, salads, desserts and drinks to create an array of culinary delights.

There are basically two ways to use tofu: boldly displayed and eaten as a food to be enjoyed for its own intrinsic qualities, or combined with other ingredients. Either way, the results can be pleasantly surprising.

Sliced, diced, blended, pureed, whipped, scrambled, crumbled, marinated, boiled, grilled, panfried, deep-fried, sautéed, smoked, steamed, frozen or eaten fresh just as it is, the list of ways to eat tofu is practically endless. And the fact that tofu is available in so many different forms means that it can be adapted to just about any form of preparation and cooking. Of course, some types of tofu are better suited to particular uses than others. Soft or silken tofu is readily whipped or pureed in smoothies or mayonnaise, or added to fillings, cakes and cheesecakes. Firmer types can substitute for feta cheese in salads, mozzarella in lasagne or on pizzas, be crumbled to imitate ground (minced) meat in patties or sliced or diced into a stir-fry. Any type can add moisture and structure to baked dishes without altering the flavor.

Although tofu has a long association with Asian flavors, it is equally adaptable to many cuisines, such as Mediterranean, Indian and Moroccan. Alternatively, tofu can be quite simply sautéed with Worcestershire, barbecue, plum, soy, oyster or teriyaki sauce, or marinated and cooked in red or white wine, rice wine, Marsala, port or fruit juice.

Why eat tofu, anyway?

Throughout much of Asia, tofu is one of the most important ways of using soybeans as a daily food. Slowly, we in the West are beginning to recognize its benefits and replace some of our high-protein, high-cholesterol animal foods with high-protein, no-cholesterol plant foods such as tofu.

Although high in protein, tofu is not just a healthy substitute for other protein-rich foods, such as eggs, meat and cheese. It has an abundance of isoflavones and phytoestrogens, is low in saturated fats, has no cholesterol, and helps prevent hardening of the arteries and some cancers, such as breast and prostate. Besides reducing the risk of heart disease, tofu is easy to digest. It is also an extremely useful food for diabetics. Research supports the theory that tofu promotes longevity and good health, as evidenced in Japan, which is one of the healthiest nations in the world.

This versatile food adapts easily to any dish, adding body and richness. It is an ideal diet food, is relatively inexpensive and, unlike meat with bones and fat, there is no waste. It is also useful for those in a hurry, because it is quick and easy to prepare into a nutritious but delicious meal. What more could you need?

tofu glossary

With so many different types of tofu available, how do you know which one to use and why? Knowing how tofu is made makes it easier to choose the appropriate type.

Making firm and soft tofu is similar to making cheese. Whole soybeans are washed and soaked in water overnight to soften, then pureed and strained. The liquid is the soy milk that will be made into tofu. The residue, *okara*, retains some nutritive value and can be added to dishes such as croquettes. The soy milk is heated, then a coagulant, such as nigari, calcium sulphate or lemon juice, is added to separate the soy milk into curds and whey. The soft curds are carefully ladled into cloth-lined boxes with small holes so the whey drips out. The curds are gently pressed to form a block of tofu. The more the block is pressed the firmer the tofu, and the more nutritious it becomes. The difference between firm and soft tofu is simply the amount of water left in the bean curd.

For silken tofu, the process is more like that for making yogurt. The coagulant firms the soy milk without separating it into curds and whey, producing a smoother and creamier texture.

It is easy to make tofu at home using utensils found in most kitchens. After soaking overnight, fresh tofu can be ready in an hour for relatively little cost. Like fresh homemade bread, fresh tofu has a rich taste and delicate flavor that is rarely matched by the commercial alternatives.

Firm and soft tofu

The two most popular types of tofu are the Chinese and Japanese style. Chinese-style tofu is coarser, more grainy and has a higher protein content than the softer, more delicate Japanese-style tofu.

Firm or regular tofu

Firm tofu is known in Japan as *momen*, or cotton, and could be considered the all-purpose tofu because it holds its shape during cooking, but is still soft enough to puree. Its creamy texture is not quite as smooth as soft tofu, but it is not as coarse as the extra firm. This is the safest, most versatile selection if you are unsure which type to use in a recipe. It is available in sealed refrigerated containers, refrigerated vacuum-sealed packs and shelf-stable cartons that require no refrigeration until opened. Although labeled firm, textures vary with different manufacturers.

Fresh tofu

Fresh tofu, or freshly-made tofu, is made by the curds and whey method. It is more commonly available in a Chinese-style, firm-textured tofu, packed in water in refrigerated containers and sold as "fresh tofu," from Asian markets.

Japanese brands tend to be smoother and have a slightly different flavor than the coarser Chinese brands. Fresh organic tofu is also available. Although it is firm, fresh tofu is suitable for most recipes because it holds its shape during cooking, but it will also puree to a smooth consistency.

Silken tofu

Made like yogurt, silken tofu sets without producing whey and is not pressed. Although it is usually slightly softer than soft tofu, because of the higher water content, the names are often interchanged. It is available in refrigerated vacuum-sealed containers and shelf-stable cartons that require no refrigeration until opened.

Silken tofu is available in soft, firm and extra-firm varieties. Although the smooth, creamy texture and delicate flavor of even the firmest silken tofu is still quite soft, it can be pan-fried, grilled or gently folded into or carefully stirred in salads and stir-fries. Soft silken tofu can be added to salads or floated in soups as is, but simmering it in lightly salted water for 2 minutes will firm the texture and develop the flavor. All of the silken tofu types puree and scramble well, although the soft exudes more liquid than others and may need to be cooked slightly longer to allow for evaporation.

Soft tofu

With its smooth, creamy texture and delicate taste, soft tofu is the one to use in simple dishes that require little handling of the tofu, as it breaks easily. It purees well and can be the basis of smoothies, dips, sauces, puddings and parfaits or added to or substituted for mayonnaise, sour cream, yogurt, milk and eggs. It is available in refrigerated vacuum-sealed packs and shelf-stable cartons that require no refrigeration until opened.

Extra-firm tofu

Just as its name describes, this type of tofu is quite firm because it has been pressed longer to expel more liquid. It holds its shape during cooking and can be shredded or crumbled like feta cheese. It can be added to salads, sprinkled over vegetables or added to falafel or other patties or to fillings such as for strudels. It is available in refrigerated vacuum-sealed packs and shelf-stable cartons that require no refrigeration until opened.

Powdered tofu (instant tofu or soy milk powder)

Now that so many types of tofu are readily available, there is not much need for powdered tofu, but it is a relatively quick and easy standby for the pantry or to use in making your own tofu. It is also lightweight and convenient for camping trips. Simply combine the sachet of tofu powder with water, heat, add the sachet of coagulant and allow to set. The texture and flavor is similar to fresh tofu.

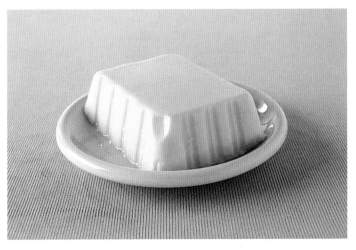

Nigari tofu

Nigari tofu is named for nigari (bittern) or refined nigari (magnesium chloride), the coagulant used in making it. Natural nigari is the traditional Japanese coagulant, and it is considered to give tofu the best flavor.

Flavored or dessert tofu

Refrigerated packets of tofu in such flavors as coconut, almond and mango are readily available from supermarkets. They can be served with fresh fruit as a quick and easy dessert, or pureed and combined with other ingredients to make smoothies, cakes, biscuits, custard or ice cream. Tofu ice cream is also available.

Grilled tofu (yaki-dofu)

Lightly grilling tofu makes the texture firmer and adds a nuttier flavor. The mottled browned surface also looks appealing. It is easy to grill tofu yourself by draining and pressing regular tofu and lightly grilling or panfrying each side over high heat. It is also available already grilled in packets and cans. *Yaki-dofu* is often used in one-pot Japanese dishes such as sukiyaki. Marinating tofu before grilling is optional.

Deep-fried tofu (age)

It is relatively easy to deep-fry tofu at home, but deep-fried tofu is readily available in a variety of shapes suitable for different cooking uses. Refrigerated and frozen packets can be found in Asian food stores, natural foods stores and some supermarkets. Thickness and shape determine the different types. Pouring boiling water over the tofu or lightly boiling it for 1 minute before use, will remove excess oil. Squeeze gently to remove the water and pat dry with paper towels.

Thin deep-fried tofu (aburaage or usuage)

Thin deep-fried tofu can be thinly sliced and added to soups, casseroles and stir-fries. They can also be split along one end, opened as a pouch and filled with a sweet or savory filling. They are available in small and large sizes in frozen packs at Asian food stores.

(Not pictured) Thick deep-fried tofu (atsuage or namaage)

This tofu is deep-fried quickly so the outside is crisp but the inside remains soft. It is available in 1-inch (2.5-cm) thick slices, small or large cubes, or triangles, in refrigerated packs in Asian food stores and some natural foods stores. Freezing adversely affects the texture.

(Right) Freeze-dried tofu (koya-dofu)

Freezing turns all the water in the bean curd to ice. When defrosted, the water drains away, leaving a lightweight sponge of beige tofu with a concentrated protein level. Freeze-dried tofu is available from Asian food stores in packets of 5 or 10 blocks, each one weighing less than 1 oz (30 g). These must be soaked in hot water until softened, about 5 minutes, and the excess liquid squeezed out before use. It can then be diced, sliced or torn into pieces so its firm, chewy texture can absorb flavored liquids during cooking. It can also be panfried or coated in crumbs and deep-fried.

Seasoned tofu pouches

These thin deep-fried tofu pouches are cooked in sweetened soy sauce and traditionally filled with sushi rice (*inari-zushi*). They are available in refrigerated vacuum packs and cans.

Tempeh

Originally from Indonesia, tempeh is still that country's most popular form of soy food. Tempeh is a cake of fermented, cooked soybeans, sometimes in combination with grains, that is held together by a white mold (mycelium). It has a mild nutty, yeastlike flavor and a texture similar to meat. The fermentation also makes it more digestible than other soy foods. It is available from Asian food stores, natural foods stores and most supermarkets in refrigerated vacuum-sealed packets.

Like tofu, tempeh is versatile and absorbs flavors, including marinades, well. It can be sliced or diced for grilling, deep-frying, panfrying or steaming. It can be used in soups, dips, wraps, sauces, and stir-fries, or eaten on its own. Spraying with cooking oil before frying prevents tempeh from absorbing too much oil and adds to its nutty flavor and crisp texture. A variety of commercially prepared and marinated tempeh products are available in supermarkets and natural foods stores. These require little, if any, preparation, making them quick and easy additions to soups, stir-fries, casseroles, sauces, and dips, or substitutes for meat in many dishes.

It's easy to create different textures, shapes and flavors using tofu because just about anything sweet or savory, and just about any fruit or vegetable, goes with it. You can add deep-fried tofu puffs to a stir-fry, float decoratively cut silken tofu in soup, crumble tofu into a salad or puree it in a smoothie. Tempeh can even be thinly sliced and panfried to make crackers. Combining different types of tofu in one dish also creates flavor and textural contrasts, as they will absorb flavors and colors differently.

Marinating tofu before cooking adds flavor. Grilling or panfrying tofu not only enhances its nutty flavor, but firms its texture. Boiling tofu for 2 minutes also firms the texture, and boiling for 5 minutes can freshen aging tofu. Adding a pinch of salt while boiling can extend the life of refrigerated tofu and prevent it becoming too hard when cooked. Freezing tofu makes the texture firmer and chewier and darkens the color.

Because tofu can mimic the texture of other foods, such as meat, eggs, fish, and chicken, people often think they are eating the real thing. Lightly coating tofu in seasoned flour, fresh or dried bread crumbs, crushed breakfast cereals or nuts and panfrying or deep-frying it also adds variety.

Many prepared tofu products have been marinated or combined with other ingredients, making their addition to dishes quick, easy and delicious. These are available in Asian food stores, natural foods stores, and supermarkets. Tofu with chopped vegetables or herbs, tempeh with ginger and soy, Thai spiced tofu, teriyaki tofu, tofu burgers, tofu frankfurters, seasoned tempeh, tofu dips and flavored tofu desserts and ice creams are just some in the range of available products.

Ingredients

Because of its mild, nutty but otherwise neutral taste, tofu combines well with just about any other flavor or ingredient, whether traditional Asian, Mediterranean, Moroccan or Indian. It can also be delicious with just a simple sauce or oil. Most of the ingredients listed here are readily available at Asian or specialty foods stores, as well as some delicatessens and supermarkets.

Oils: Ghee, olive oil, peanut oil, and Asian sesame oil.

Herbs and spices: Basil, cayenne, chili, chives, cilantro (fresh coriander), cumin, curry leaves and powder, garlic, ginger, kaffir lime leaves, lemongrass, mint, Szechwan pepper, tamarind, Thai basil, turmeric, and umeboshi (pickled Japanese plums).

Stocks, sauces and seasonings: Black and white sesame seeds, shaoxing wine, coconut milk or cream, dashi broth (made with konbu seaweed and bonito fish flakes; instant dashi granules are available in Asian food stores), hoisin sauce, Indian chutneys and relishes, ketjap manis (sweet soy sauce), mirin, miso, nam pla (fermented fish sauce), Parmesan cheese, preserved lemons, oyster sauce, plum sauce, rice vinegar, sake, sambal oelek (red chili paste), shrimp paste, soy sauce, sweet chili sauce, tamarind, wasabi paste, and Worcestershire sauce.

Noodles: Egg noodles, mung bean noodles, rice noodles, and soba, somen and udon noodles.

Others: Nori and other seaweeds.

Selecting and storing tofu

Tofu is widely available from Asian food stores, natural foods stores and most supermarkets. Label descriptions and textures can vary between different manufacturers, so experiment to see which types and brands best suit your needs.

In general, firm and extra-firm Chinese-style tofu is best for stir-fries, kabobs or dishes that require tofu to hold its shape. However, some brands will be much firmer than others, some will puree well and some will crumble to resemble feta cheese. Whether Japanese-style silken tofu is soft or firm, it can hold its shape in soups and even some stir-fries if handled very carefully. It purees well to use for dips, salad dressings, drinks and sauces and to replace dairy products, such as sour cream, in some dishes.

Tofu is available in refrigerated plastic containers, refrigerated vacuum-sealed packs or shelf-stable sealed cartons that require no refrigeration until opened. Once opened, all tofu must be kept refrigerated in sealed containers covered with water that is changed daily. It should be used within 5–7 days if not frozen. Tofu can be frozen for up to 3 months, but the texture will be firmer and coarser, and the color may darken. Tofu should smell slightly sweet. Discard it if it smells sour, feels slippery or is tinged with pink or green. Deep-fried tofu will keep for about 10 days; seasoned tofu should be used within 3–4 days.

Once opened, tempeh should be used within 5 days, or frozen for up to 3 months. If gray or black spots appear, caused by the active mold, just cut them off, but discard any tempeh that feels slippery or smells of ammonia.

Freezing and defrosting tofu

Tofu can be frozen, and even used in cooking while still frozen, but the texture becomes firmer and more crumbly and the color darkens slightly. As the water in the tofu freezes, it expands to form small pockets. When the tofu thaws and the water drains away, the pockets remain, giving the tofu a crumbly texture and the ability to absorb flavors like a sponge. Especially when cut into pieces, these small pores allow the tofu to absorb more flavor from marinades and sauces. If crumbled, defrosted tofu resembles ground meat. A similar texture can be achieved by breaking up a firm or extra-firm block of tofu and stir-frying it in a splash of oil until it is dry.

Freezing silken tofu is not recommended, as freezing ruins the delicate texture.

Defrost tofu quickly by puncturing holes in the top of the plastic container and microwaving it for 5–7 minutes. It can also be defrosted in warm water, and the excess moisture gently squeezed out. Tofu can be defrosted at room temperature, which should take about 3 hours, but ideally it should be thawed overnight in the refrigerator. Drain and press thawed tofu before use to expel any excess liquid.

Tempeh can be defrosted by microwaving it on high for 45 to 60 seconds or leaving it in the refrigerator overnight.

How to cut tofu

Tofu can be sliced, diced, crumbled or cut into decorative shapes with a melon baller or biscuit cutter.

How to cut tofu

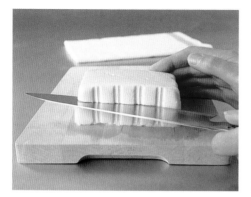 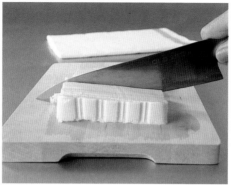 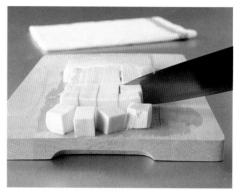

1. Cut a block of tofu in half horizontally into 1 or 2 slices.

2. Cut vertically into strips of required thickness.

3. Give block a quarter turn and, holding tofu gently, slice to make cubes.

Making a chrysanthemum flower

1. Place a chopstick on each side of a block of tofu and cut into strips that are ³/₈–³/₄ inch (1–2 cm) thick. Chopsticks will stop knife cutting completely through tofu. Turn block and chopsticks 90 degrees and repeat.

2. Cut tofu block with a biscuit cutter to make a round shape. Tofu can be left in water until needed, then gently opened out like flower stamens.

How to remove excess moisture

Removing excess moisture from tofu makes room for other liquids, such as marinades and sauces, to be absorbed and prevents excess liquid from diluting sauces and dressings. It also prevents tofu from spattering when frying.

Draining
The first step is simply pouring off the water that surrounds the tofu in the packet. Further draining can be done in a colander.

Pressing
Although not necessary for firm and extra-firm tofu, pressing tofu before use removes even more moisture and makes the tofu firmer and less watery. The simplest method for pressing tofu is to wrap it in paper towels, place 2 dinner plates on top and leave it to drain for 20–30 minutes, or longer for a drier, firmer texture. Alternatively, place tofu between 2 cutting boards that are tilted at a 45-degree angle (rest boards on an upturned bowl). Put a weight, such as a can of vegetables, on top and leave to drain into the sink for 20–30 minutes. Pat tofu dry before cooking.

Patting dry
Place sliced or diced tofu on a paper towel, cover with another paper towel layer and gently pat to absorb any excess surface moisture before cooking.

Pan drying
Slice or dice drained tofu and heat it in a nonstick or lightly greased frying pan over a medium-high heat. Any excess moisture will evaporate and the tofu will brown lightly, giving it a slightly nutty flavor and firmer texture.

Oven drying
Place sliced or diced tofu in a lightly greased dish and bake in a moderately hot oven (375°F/190°C) until excess moisture is released, 5–10 minutes. Drain, then return tofu to the oven to evaporate any remaining moisture and firm the texture.

Grill drying
Place sliced or diced tofu under a preheated broiler (grill) and heat until lightly browned, about 5 minutes on each side. Besides evaporating any excess liquid, the texture will be firmer and the browning will bring out a nutty flavor. Grilled tofu is also available in cans and refrigerated packs.

1. Pour off water that surrounds tofu in package.

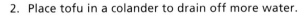

2. Place tofu in a colander to drain off more water.

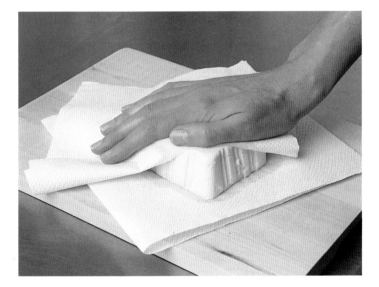

3. Wrap tofu in paper towels.

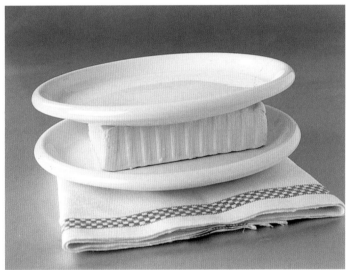

4. Place 2 dinner plates on top of wrapped tofu and let drain for 20–30 minutes, or longer for a drier, firmer texture.

How to change soft tofu into firm

Some recipes require firm or extra-firm tofu. If all you have is soft tofu, it's an easy matter to make it firm:

1. If tofu does not need to retain its shape, put soft tofu in a clean dish towel, then twist and squeeze it to remove excess liquid. Leave it to drain in a colander for a few minutes.

2. If tofu is to be sliced or diced, wrap block of tofu in paper towels.

3. Press wrapped block of tofu between 2 cutting boards with a weight on top.

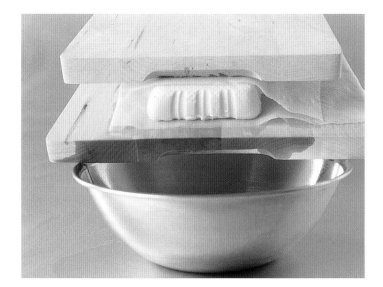

4. Slope boards at 45 degrees by resting one end on an upturned bowl to allow liquid to drain into sink. The longer tofu is pressed, the firmer the texture.

5. Soft tofu can also be firmed by boiling it. Chop tofu into even cubes and place in boiling water.

6. Boil tofu cubes gently for 2 minutes. Drain.

7. Although a block of firm tofu cannot be made into soft, pureeing it with some extra water gives it a softer, creamier texture that is suitable for drinks, sauces and dressings.

How to prepare tofu for cooking

Marinating

Marinating tofu is a simple way of giving it flavor. With unpressed tofu, marinades don't penetrate deeper than the surface, so it's necessary to marinate it for only a short time. Cutting the tofu so it has a larger exposed surface allows more flavor to be absorbed. If tofu is drained and pressed, it will absorb more marinade.

Using a marinade as a cooking liquid is an effective way to infuse tofu with flavor, as the liquid reduces and thickens while the tofu cooks. Simply slice or dice the tofu, spray a hot frying pan or grill pan with cooking-oil spray and sear the tofu until golden on both sides. Then pour the marinade over the tofu and heat until the liquid caramelizes.

Grilling

Grill drained and pressed regular tofu, or panfry each side in a nonstick frying pan over medium-high heat. Grilled tofu is often used in one-pot Japanese dishes such as sukiyaki and is available in cans or packets. The tofu can be sliced and marinated or brushed with a favorite sauce, such as Worcestershire, soy sauce, barbecue or teriyaki sauce before grilling, or served with a dipping sauce. Grill the tofu quickly so it doesn't dry out and sauce doesn't burn. Serve topped with fish or shellfish, vegetables, chutneys, sliced onions or sliced apples.

Pureeing or blending

Pureed tofu can be substituted for or added to mayonnaise, cream, sour cream or yogurt and can be used virtually unnoticed in soups, shakes, sauces, dressings, dips, and casseroles. Silken and soft tofu are the best types to puree. If firmer types are used, it may be necessary to add a bit of water to achieve a creamy consistency.

Parboiling/braising

Parboiling tofu, especially soft or silken, in water will firm its texture. Bring 6 cups of water or broth to a boil in a large pan. Add the tofu with a pinch of salt (optional) and simmer for 1–2 minutes for diced tofu or 4–5 minutes for larger pieces. Drain and pat dry with paper towels before frying. If tofu is simmered in stock or a sauce, it will absorb the flavors and color.

Panfrying/stir-frying

Frying tofu in a little oil is a good alternative to deep-frying and gives it a crisp, golden exterior while the inside stays soft. Pat the tofu dry with paper towels. Heat enough oil to film the bottom of a frying pan over medium heat. Add the tofu and fry until golden, about 5 minutes on each side. Soy or teriyaki sauce can be added near the end of cooking to caramelize onto the tofu before serving. Serve as a finger food, or with a salad, add to other dishes or combine with vegetables, meat, fish or shellfish, herbs and sauces in the pan to make a quick and easy main meal.

Scrambling

Scrambled tofu resembles scrambled eggs. The more the tofu is stirred, the more it will break up. Firm or soft tofu can be used, but soft tofu may release more liquid and require increased cooking time or temperature to allow for evaporation. Add vegetables, fresh herbs and/or sauces for a quick and easy meal.

Steaming

Steamed tofu stays moist and soft. Marinating the tofu first will add flavor. Put tofu in a steamer basket over a pot of simmering liquid, cover with a tight-fitting lid and steam until heated through.

Deep-frying (preparing age)

Deep-frying has been out of favor for many people in recent years, but if correctly done, the food will be crisp on the outside and soft and moist on the inside and very little oil will be absorbed. Tofu must be drained, pressed and dried with paper towels before deep-frying so the excess liquid does not spatter in the oil. Firm and extra-firm tofu are the best types to deep-fry. Fill a deep-sided saucepan or wok one-third full of peanut, vegetable or canola oil and heat over medium heat to 365°F (185°C). Add several sliced or diced pieces of tofu and fry until golden, being careful the pieces do not stick together. Do not add too many pieces at once or the oil temperature will drop too low, causing the tofu to absorb excess oil. Remove from oil with tongs or chopsticks and drain on paper towels. Serve with salt and pepper or a dipping sauce, or add to other dishes.

Smoking

Smoked tofu is available from Asian food stores, natural foods stores and some supermarkets, but it is easy to do your own. Drain firm or extra-firm tofu, press it and dry it with paper towels, then slice it. Brush the slices with oil combined with a favorite sauce (soy, Worcestershire, barbecue, ketjap manis) or spice rub. Light a charcoal fire in an outdoor grill. When the coals are glowing, add a couple of tablespoons of soaked and drained wood chips. Put tofu on a lightly oiled rack above the coals. Cover the grill and smoke for 15 minutes. Brush the slices with more sauce and grill 15 minutes longer. The tofu should be firm but not hard. Serve hot or cold with a dipping sauce, in salads, or top with meat or vegetables.

How to reconstitute freeze-dried tofu

Cover tofu with warm water and stand until reconstituted, about 5 minutes. Gently squeeze out excess water and pat dry with paper towels before using.

How to prepare deep-fried tofu for cooking

Pour boiling water over deep-fried tofu pouches or puffs before use to remove excess oil. Alternatively, drop tofu into boiling water for 1 minute. Drain and let cool slightly. Squeeze out excess water and pat dry with paper towels before use.

Substituting tofu in recipes

Tofu can add moisture and structure to baked dishes without altering their flavor. When using in baked dishes, be sure the tofu is pureed until smooth or the tofu bits will harden as they cook, which will look and taste unappetizing. Substitute about 1/4 cup (2 fl oz/60 ml) pureed silken tofu for each egg in pancakes, muffins, quick breads and cake recipes, or add tofu with eggs or egg whites. Soy milk can be used instead of cows' milk in many dishes, although the color of the dish may be slightly darker and dishes will brown more readily. If using tofu as a meat or chicken substitute, just replace 1 lb (500 g) meat with 1 lb firm or extra-firm tofu. If substituting ground (minced) meat, freezing the tofu first before crumbling will make it look even more like meat.

Deep-fried tofu in broth

Agedashi dofu

20 oz (600 g) silken firm tofu, drained and
  pressed (see pages 18–19)

2 tablespoons cornstarch (cornflour)

vegetable or sunflower oil for deep-frying

³/₄ cup (6 fl oz/180 ml) dashi stock

2¹/₂ tablespoons soy sauce

2¹/₂ tablespoons mirin

¹/₄ cup (2 oz/60 g) shredded daikon

1 tablespoon grated fresh ginger

1 scallion (shallot/spring onion), green part only

1 tablespoon fine bonito flakes (katsuobushi)

Agedashi dofu is a classic Japanese tofu dish. Bite-sized blocks of tofu, deep-fried until lightly crisp, are served with a seasoned dashi broth and simple condiments of ginger, scallion and bonito flakes.

Cut tofu into 12 equal cubes. Toss in cornstarch, shaking off any excess. Fill a frying pan or wok one-third full with oil and heat to 365°F (185°C). Deep-fry tofu in batches until lightly browned all over, 5–6 minutes. Drain on paper towels.

In a small saucepan, combine broth, soy sauce and mirin and bring to a simmer. Place 3 pieces of tofu in each serving bowl. Arrange daikon, ginger and onion on top and pour sauce around tofu. Sprinkle with bonito flakes and serve immediately.

Serves 4

Variation

Season cornstarch with chili pepper flakes, fresh herbs, or black and white sesame seeds.

DEEP-FRIED TOFU IN BROTH

Smoked-trout mousse with tofu crackers

FOR TOFU CRACKERS

5 oz (150 g) firm tofu, drained

vegetable or sunflower oil for deep-frying

2 smoked trout (about 1 lb/500 g)

4 oz (125 g) soft tofu, drained

juice of 1 lemon

1 teaspoon Dijon mustard

4 tablespoons (2 oz/60 g) butter, melted

1 bunch chives, finely chopped

2 tablespoons finely chopped fresh dill

1 medium green chili pepper, seeded and finely chopped (optional)

To make tofu crackers: Cut firm tofu into slices ¼ inch (6 mm) thick. Pat dry with paper towels. Fill a frying pan or wok one-third full with oil and heat to 365°F (185°C). Deep-fry slices until golden brown and crunchy, about 2 minutes. Drain on paper towels. Store in an airtight container when cool, but use within 2 days.

Remove skin and bones from trout, checking carefully that no fine bones have been left in flesh. In a food processor, puree tofu. Add trout, lemon juice, mustard and butter and puree until smooth. Stir in chives, dill and chili pepper. Pour into small bowls or soufflé dishes and refrigerate. Serve in pots with tofu crackers.

Makes 2 cups (1 lb/500 g); serves 6–8

Tip

Add a small quantity of mousse to an omelette just before folding it in half.

Variation

Substitute smoked or canned salmon or crabmeat for the trout. Substitute sweet chili sauce for the mustard.

SMOKED-TROUT MOUSSE WITH TOFU CRACKERS

Tofu bruschetta

4 slices soy and linseed bread (available from
    natural foods stores) or preferred bread
garlic oil (see note)
2¹/₂ oz (75 g) extra-firm or firm tofu, drained
1 large tomato, chopped
1¹/₂ tablespoons balsamic vinegar
2 tablespoons finely chopped fresh parsley
14-16 semi sun-dried tomatoes packed in oil,
    drained and chopped
¹/₃ cup (3 fl oz/90 ml) basil pesto (page 52)

Lightly brush both sides of bread with oil. Preheat broiler (grill) and cook bread until golden and crunchy, 2–3 minutes each side. Crumble tofu between fingers until it resembles coarse crumbs. In a medium bowl, combine tomato, vinegar, parsley and semi sun-dried tomatoes. Spread a layer of pesto on each bread slice and top with the tomato mixture. Serve immediately.

Makes 4 slices

Note: To make garlic oil, crush 2 garlic cloves with flat side of a knife blade. Combine with 1 cup (8 fl oz/250 ml) olive oil and keep in an airtight container to use as required. Also available from supermarkets.

Beet and orange dip

2 medium beets (beetroot), 5 oz (150 g) each
4 oz (125 g) silken tofu, drained
1 clove garlic, minced
1 tablespoon fresh lemon juice
2 tablespoons chopped fresh chives
2 tablespoons chopped fresh mint
salt and pepper
4 drops Tabasco or other vinegar-based hot sauce
grated zest and juice of 1 orange
1 tablespoon prepared horseradish

Trim stalks from beets, leaving 1 inch (2.5 cm) attached. Put beets in a large saucepan and cover with water. Bring water to a boil, reduce heat and simmer until beets are tender, about 30 minutes. Let cool, peel, then shred or finely chop them.

In a food processor, puree tofu until smooth. Add garlic and lemon juice and puree until combined, about 15 seconds. Pour tofu mixture into a large bowl and add beets, chives, mint, salt, pepper and Tabasco. Divide mixture in half. Add orange juice and zest to one half and horseradish to the other. Refrigerate until required. Serve as a dip with crisp vegetable sticks, such as carrot, celery, and bell pepper (capsicum) and/or crackers. Garnish with fresh parsley.

Makes about 1¹/₂ cups (12 oz/375 ml)

TOFU BRUSCHETTA

Crunchy tofu with creamy sweet chili sauce

4 blocks (2 oz/60 g) freeze-dried tofu,
  reconstituted (see page 23)

1 cup (8 fl oz/250 ml) water

1/4 cup (2 fl oz/60 ml) soy sauce

1 teaspoon grated fresh ginger

2 tablespoons mirin or sweet white wine

1/4 cup (1 1/2 oz/45 g) all-purpose (plain) flour

2 eggs, lightly beaten with 2 tablespoons water

3/4 cup (2 oz/60 g) crushed, shredded-wheat
  breakfast cereal

vegetable or sunflower oil for frying

FOR CREAMY SWEET CHILI SAUCE

3 1/2 oz (105 g) soft tofu, drained

1/4 cup (2 fl oz/60 ml) sweet chili sauce

1 teaspoon soy sauce

1 teaspoon chopped cilantro (coriander) leaves

Gently squeeze most of liquid out of reconstituted freeze-dried tofu. In a medium saucepan, combine tofu, water, soy sauce, ginger and mirin. Gradually bring to a boil, reduce heat and simmer for 15 minutes, turning tofu occasionally. Remove from heat and let cool for 5 minutes. Squeeze excess moisture from tofu. Cut tofu into strips 1/2 inch (12 mm) thick and lightly dust them with flour. Dip strips into egg mixture, draining off any excess, then roll them in crushed wheat flakes.

Fill a deep saucepan or wok one-third full with oil and heat to 365°F (185°C). Deep-fry tofu in batches until golden, 2–3 minutes. Drain on paper towels and serve immediately, with chili sauce.

To make creamy sweet chili sauce: In a blender, puree soft tofu until smooth. Add chili sauce, soy sauce and cilantro and mix until well combined.

Serves 4

Variation

Dice tofu before coating and frying and serve on toothpicks as party food.

Hazelnut and tofu balls with spicy plum sauce

FOR SPICY PLUM SAUCE

1/2 cup (4 fl oz/125 ml) plum sauce

2 tablespoons sweet chili sauce

1 teaspoon soy sauce

2 teaspoons water

4 oz (125 g) firm or extra-firm tofu, drained

1/2 cup (2 oz/60 g) toasted ground hazelnuts

1 small onion, finely chopped

1/2 cup (2 oz/60 g) dried bread crumbs

1 egg, lightly beaten

2 tablespoons chopped fresh parsley

salt and pepper to taste

vegetable or sunflower oil for deep-frying

To make spicy plum sauce: Combine all ingredients in a small bowl, stirring until well combined. Set aside.

Using your fingers, crumble tofu until it resembles coarse bread crumbs. In a large bowl, combine tofu, hazelnuts, onion, bread crumbs, egg, parsley, salt and pepper. Shape mixture into 1 1/2-inch (4-cm) balls.

Fill a wok or frying pan one-third full with oil and heat to 350°F (180°C). Fry tofu balls until golden, 3–4 minutes. Serve immediately, with dipping sauce.

Makes 20 balls

Variations

Shape mixture into patties and slice to use as a filling for lavash or pita pockets with spicy plum sauce, butter lettuce and snow pea sprouts.

Serve tofu balls with pasta and fresh tomato sauce (page 72) as a main course.

HAZELNUT AND TOFU BALLS WITH SPICY PLUM SAUCE   3 3

Crispy red curry puffs with herbed coconut sauce

FOR HERBED COCONUT SAUCE

1/2 cup (4 fl oz/125 ml) thick coconut cream

2 tablespoons chopped fresh mint

2 tablespoons chopped cilantro (fresh coriander) leaves

3 1/2 oz (105 g) firm or extra-firm tofu, drained and shredded

1/3 cup (1 oz/30 g) fresh soy and linseed bread crumbs

1 scallion (shallot/spring onion), green part only, finely chopped

1 garlic clove, finely chopped

2 tablespoons Thai red curry paste

12 large deep-fried tofu puffs

1/4 cup (2 fl oz/60 ml) ketjap manis

To make coconut sauce: Mix coconut cream, mint and cilantro, stirring until well combined. Set aside.

Preheat oven to 400°F (200°C). Lightly grease a baking sheet or line it with parchment (baking) paper.

In a large bowl, combine tofu, bread crumbs, scallion, garlic and curry paste. Cut each tofu puff in half diagonally and make a pocket inside with fingers. Fill each puff with about 1 teaspoon tofu mixture. Brush each puff, including filling, with ketjap manis. Place puffs on baking sheet and bake until crisp and lightly browned, 8–10 minutes. Serve with herbed coconut sauce for dipping.

Makes 24 puffs

Tip

Soy and linseed bread is available from health foods stores and some supermarkets.

light meals

Mini salmon frittatas

2 large potatoes, peeled and cut into ¹/₂-inch
(12-mm) cubes

2 tablespoons olive oil

1 leek, white part only, cleaned and chopped

4 oz (125 g) firm or silken firm tofu, drained

4 oz (125 g) extra-firm tofu, drained and coarsely
shredded

¹/₂ lb (250 g) salmon fillet

4 eggs, lightly beaten

1 tablespoon chopped fresh dill

1 tablespoon chopped fresh chives

salt and pepper to taste

2 thin deep-fried tofu (aburaage)

1 tablespoon finely chopped fresh parsley

Boil, steam or microwave potatoes until cooked through, 8–10 minutes, and leave to cool.

In a frying pan, heat olive oil over medium-low heat and cook leeks, without browning, until tender, about 5 minutes. Remove from heat and let cool.

In a food processor, puree silken tofu until smooth. Thinly slice salmon and cut into 1-inch (2.5-cm) pieces. In a food processor, process deep-fried tofu until it resembles coarse bread crumbs.

In a large bowl, combine potatoes, leeks, silken and firm tofu, salmon, eggs, dill, chives, salt and pepper. Spoon mixture into lightly greased muffin cups. Sprinkle with crumbled tofu and parsley. Bake in moderate oven (350°F/180°C) until cooked through, 12–15 minutes. Serve hot or cold with a tossed salad.

Makes 12 frittatas

Variations

Substitute smoked or well drained canned salmon, for fresh salmon and omit the salt.

Bake a single frittata in a baking dish and cut into squares or wedges to serve.

MINI SALMON FRITTATAS

Tofu wraps

a selection of wrappers such as lavash, pita (Lebanese bread) and roti (Indian flat bread)

Arrange a selection of wrappers on a platter and serve with a choice of fillings so that guests can help themselves.

Fillings

1. Hazelnut and tofu balls with:
- spicy plum sauce (page 32) and shredded lettuce
- hummus and tabbouleh
- yogurt-cucumber sauce (page 54) and mesculin (baby salad leaves)
- mango salsa (see page 42).

2. Tempeh brushed with teriyaki sauce and panfried. Serve with Beet and orange dip (page 28).

3. Lime and wasabi tofu (page 64) and shredded grilled chicken with avocado.

4. Pork and tofu triangles (variation, page 40) with yogurt-cucumber sauce (page 54).

Note: Sliced English (hothouse) cucumber, arugula (rocket), sliced yellow bell pepper (capsicum) and shredded carrot can be added to all of the above combinations.

Grilled tofu with tahini and spinach miso

1/2 cup (5 oz/150 g) white (shiro) miso

3 teaspoons sugar

2 tablespoons mirin

1/4 cup (2 fl oz/60 ml) chicken or dashi stock

2 tablespoons tahini (sesame paste)

2 cups (2 oz/60 g) firmly packed spinach leaves

20 oz (600 g) firm tofu, well drained (see
   pages 18–19)

lemon zest curls for garnish

In a small saucepan, mix miso, sugar, mirin and stock and heat until sugar dissolves, stirring occasionally. Stir in tahini. Blanch spinach in boiling water for 1 minute, then drain well, squeezing out excess water. In a blender, puree spinach with half of miso mixture.

Cut tofu into 3/4-inch (2-cm) thick slices. Preheat a broiler (grill), place tofu slices on a lightly greased overn tray and cook over high heat until lightly browned, 1–2 minutes on each side. Spread half of tofu slices with spinach–miso mixture and other half with plain miso mixture. Cook until lightly browned, 2–3 minutes. Garnish with lemon zest and serve with a tossed salad.

Serves 4–6

Tofu-tempeh hummus

5 1/2 oz (170 g) tempeh

5 1/2 oz (170 g) soft or silken firm tofu, drained

1/3 cup (3 fl oz/90 ml) fresh lemon juice

1/4 cup (2 fl oz/60 ml) tahini (sesame paste)

1/4 teaspoon salt

2 garlic cloves, finely chopped

In a food processor, puree tempeh and tofu until fairly smooth. Add all remaining ingredients and process until smooth. Serve as a sauce with grilled fish in wraps and sandwiches, or as a dip with crackers or crisp vegetable sticks. To store, cover and refrigerate for up to 3 days.

Makes about 2 cups (13 oz/400 g)

Pork and tofu triangles

½ lb (250 g) ground (minced) pork or chicken

2 tablespoons finely sliced scallion
   (shallot/spring onion)

1 tablespoon sake

¼ teaspoon Asian sesame oil

2 teaspoons potato flour or cornstarch
   (cornflour)

1 tablespoon Japanese soy sauce

½ teaspoon grated fresh ginger

2 blocks firm tofu, 10 oz (300 g) each, drained
   and pressed (see pages 18–19)

cornstarch (cornflour) for coating

vegetable or sunflower oil for deep-frying

mixed salad greens, for serving

soy sauce, serving

In a medium bowl, combine pork, scallion, sake, sesame oil, potato flour, soy sauce and ginger. Mix well.

Cut tofu blocks in half, then cut each half diagonally to make 4 triangles. Scoop out a small spoonful of tofu on long diagonal side of each triangle and stuff opening with meat mixture, being careful not to break tofu. Roll each triangle in cornstarch.

Fill a frying pan or wok with oil one-third full and heat to 365°F (185°C) and deep-fry triangles, until golden and meat is cooked, 2–3 minutes on each side. Turn tofu carefully so it doesn't break. Drain on paper towels and serve immediately with salad greens and extra soy sauce.

Makes 8 triangles

Variations

Flavor the cornstarch for coating the triangles with curry powder or chili pepper flakes.

Omit cornstarch coating and dip tofu into lightly beaten egg, then roll in coarse bread crumbs.

PORK AND TOFU TRIANGLES

Tandoori mushrooms with mango salsa

FOR MANGO SALSA

1 small mango, peeled and finely diced

1 scallion (shallot/spring onion), sliced

2 teaspoons chopped cilantro (fresh coriander) leaves

1/4 teaspoon grated fresh ginger

1 tablespoon finely chopped fresh mint

12 large button mushrooms, stems removed

1 teaspoon salt

2 teaspoons fresh lemon juice

FOR TANDOORI STUFFING

1 teaspoon vegetable or sunflower oil

1 1/2 oz (45 g) red (Spanish) onion, finely chopped

1 tablespoon tandoori paste

1/3 cup (1 1/2 oz/45 g) finely diced red bell pepper (capsicum)

2 oz (60 g) firm tofu, drained

vegetable-oil cooking oil spray

To make mango salsa: Combine all salsa ingredients in a medium bowl. Set aside. In a bowl, toss mushrooms with salt and lemon juice and let stand for 10 minutes.

To make stuffing: In a medium frying pan, heat oil over medium heat and sauté onion for 2–3 minutes. Add tandoori paste and bell pepper and sauté for 2 minutes. Add tofu and sauté for 1–2 minutes to heat through. Remove from heat and fill mushrooms with stuffing. Spray filled mushrooms lightly with oil and bake in a moderate oven (375°F/190°C) until browned, about 10 minutes. Serve with mango salsa.

TANDOORI MUSHROOMS WITH MANGO SALSA

Tempeh patties with creamed spinach

olive-oil cooking spray

1 small red bell pepper (capsicum), seeded and thickly sliced

4 portobello flat mushrooms, stemmed and sliced

1/2 cup (2 oz/60 g) chopped walnuts

1 clove garlic, minced

1/3 cup (1 1/2 oz/45 g) grated Parmesan cheese

1/2 lb (250 g) tempeh, pureed

1/3 cup (1/2 oz/15 g) finely chopped fresh parsley

1/3 cup (1/2 oz/15 g) finely chopped fresh mint

2 small red chili peppers, seeded and finely chopped

1/4 teaspoon salt

1/4 teaspoon pepper

5 oz (150 g) extra-firm tofu, shredded

1 1/2 cups (3 oz/90 g) fresh bread crumbs

1 egg, lightly beaten

3 oz (90 g) soft tofu, drained and pureed

1/4 cup (1 1/2 oz/45 g) all-purpose (plain) flour

2 tablespoons olive oil

FOR CREAMED SPINACH

4 cups (4 oz/125 g) spinach leaves, rinsed

4 oz (125 g) soft or silken firm tofu, drained

1 garlic clove, finely chopped

1/4 cup (1/3 oz/10 g) finely chopped fresh mint

1/4 cup (2 oz/60 g) tahini (sesame paste)

1 tablespoon fresh lemon juice

1/2 teaspoon ground nutmeg

salt and pepper to taste

Heat a large frying pan over medium heat. Spray pan with cooking oil and sauté bell peppers and mushrooms until soft, about 10 minutes. Remove from pan and set aside.

In a food processor, combine walnuts, garlic, Parmesan, tempeh, parsley, mint, chili peppers, salt and pepper and process until combined, about 20 seconds. Transfer to a bowl and add shredded tofu, bread crumbs, egg and pureed tofu, stirring well to combine. Using 1/4 cup (2 oz/60 g) of mixture for each, shape into patties and lightly dust with flour. In a large frying pan over medium heat, heat oil and fry patties until golden, 3–4 minutes on each side. Serve with creamed spinach and garnish with bell peppers and mushrooms.

To make creamed spinach: In a saucepan, bring water to a boil and blanch spinach until just wilted, 2–3 minutes. Remove and drain in a sieve, pressing with back of a large spoon. In a blender, puree spinach with remaining ingredients. Transfer to a medium saucepan and heat over low heat.

Serves 4

TEMPEH PATTIES WITH CREAMED SPINACH

Grilled marinated tofu

Dengaku

1 lb (500 g) firm tofu, drained and pressed
(see pages 18–19)

1/4 cup (2 fl oz/60 ml) soy sauce

2 tablespoons water

3 tablespoons mirin

1/2 teaspoon Asian sesame oil

lime for serving

Dengaku is one of Japan's favorite and simplest ways of serving tofu. Firm, bite-sized pieces or slices of tofu are delicious and nutritious snacks when lightly grilled until golden, spread with miso or other toppings and lightly grilled again until fragrant.

Marinating the tofu before grilling adds extra flavor. Teriyaki sauce, barbecue sauce, plum sauce, ketjap manis or sweet and sour sauce, may be used as marinades, but you may need to grill the tofu for a shorter time to keep the sugar in the marinade from burning.

Cut tofu into bite-sized cubes and place in a flat dish or broiler (grill) pan. Combine soy sauce, water, mirin and sesame oil and pour over tofu. Marinate for 15 minutes, turning occasionally. Drain and pat dry with paper towels. Place tofu on a lightly greased broiler (grill) pan and cook until lightly browned, 3–4 minutes on each side. Skewer a piece of tofu and a piece of lime onto toothpicks and serve.

Serves 4

Variations

Dice tofu into 1/2-inch (12-mm) thick slices.

Lightly dust tofu with cornstarch (cornflour) or roll in beaten egg and bread crumbs, and deep-fry for a crisper texture.

Add minced garlic, grated ginger, chili pepper, Szechwan pepper, or orange or lime zest to the marinade.

GRILLED MARINATED TOFU

Sweet potato, carrot and ginger soup with soy toast

FOR SOY TOAST

4 slices soy and linseed bread (available from natural foods stores)

vegetable-oil cooking oil spray

2 tablespoons olive oil

1 medium yellow (brown) onion, chopped

14 oz (440 g) sweet potato, peeled and chopped

3 large carrots, chopped

3 teaspoons grated fresh ginger

2 small red chili peppers, seeded and finely chopped

1 tablespoon finely chopped cilantro (fresh coriander) stems

4 cups (32 fl oz/1 L) chicken stock

1 tablespoon soy sauce

10 oz (300 g) soft tofu, drained

salt and pepper to taste

1 tablespoon finely chopped cilantro (fresh coriander) leaves

To make soy toast: Lightly spray both sides of bread with oil and place under a preheated broiler (grill). Broil (grill) until lightly browned, 2–3 minutes on each side. Cut into triangles or strips.

In a large frying pan, heat oil over medium heat. Add onion, sweet potato and carrot and sauté, stirring occasionally, until softened but not browned, 7–10 minutes. Add ginger, chili peppers, cilantro stems, stock and soy sauce and bring to a boil. Reduce heat and simmer for 15 minutes.

In a food processor, puree tofu and add gradually to soup. Puree soup in batches until smooth. Add salt and pepper. Pour soup into bowls, garnish with cilantro and serve immediately with soy toast.

Serves 4

Note

The sweet potato gives this recipe a rich orange color. Sweet potato can also be known as yams or kumara.

SWEET POTATO, CARROT AND GINGER SOUP

Creamy sweet pea, potato and leek soup with tempeh crisps

FOR TEMPEH CRISPS

2¹/₂ oz (75 g) tempeh

vegetable or sunflower oil for frying

2 tablespoons olive oil

1 clove garlic, finely chopped

2 medium leeks (white part only), rinsed and
   thinly sliced

4 potatoes (1 lb/500 g), peeled and diced

6 cups (48 fl oz/1.5 L) chicken stock

¹/₄ teaspoon salt

1¹/₂ cups (8 oz/250 g) fresh or frozen peas

5 oz (150 g) silken firm or silken soft tofu, drained

cracked black pepper to taste

2 tablespoons finely chopped fresh parsley

To make tempeh crisps: Thinly slice tempeh into matchsticks. Fill a small saucepan or frying pan one-third full with oil. Heat over medium-high heat and fry tempeh until crisp. Drain on paper towels.

In a large saucepan, heat oil over medium heat. Sauté garlic and leeks until soft and just beginning to brown, about 5 minutes. Add potatoes, stock and salt, cover and simmer until potatoes are cooked through, about 8 minutes. Add peas and simmer 5–6 minutes. Remove from heat, place in a blender and puree in batches with tofu until smooth. Return to heat to warm if serving hot, or refrigerate if serving chilled. To serve, garnish with black pepper, parsley and tempeh strips.

Serves 4–6

Tip

Tempeh strips can be made 1 day ahead. Store in an airtight container.

CREAMY SWEET PEA. POTATO AND LEEK SOUP

Tomato and tofu tart with basil pesto

FOR BASIL PESTO

2 cups (2 oz/60 g) firmly packed basil, washed
   and dried

1 clove garlic, crushed

$^3/_4$ cup (4 oz/125 g) pine nuts, toasted (see note)

$^1/_3$ cup (3 fl oz/90 ml) olive oil

$^1/_3$ cup (1$^1/_2$ oz/45 g) grated Parmesan cheese

salt and pepper to taste

5$^1/_2$ oz (170 g) extra-firm or firm tofu, drained

$^1/_4$ cup (1$^1/_2$ oz/45 g) semi sun-dried tomatoes
   packed in oil, drained and chopped

1 tablespoon balsamic vinegar

1 sheet thawed frozen puff pastry, halved

2 large tomatoes, cut into thin wedges

3 scallions (shallots/spring onions), chopped

To make basil pesto: In a food processor, combine basil, garlic, and nuts and puree until smooth. With machine running, gradually add oil in a steady stream. Add Parmesan and salt and pepper to taste. Makes about 1$^1/_2$ cups (12 fl oz/375 g).

Crumble tofu until it resembles coarse crumbs. In a small bowl, combine tofu, semi sun-dried tomatoes and vinegar. Set aside.

Preheat oven to 425°F (220°C). Lightly grease a baking sheet, or line it with parchment (baking) paper. Place pastry sheet halves on prepared pan and fold up $^3/8$ inch (1 cm) on each side to form a rim. Prick base of pastry with a fork and bake until lightly browned, about 8 minutes.

Spread $^1/4$ cup (2 fl oz/60 ml) pesto over each baked pastry. Arrange half tomato wedges on top of each and sprinkle with half of tofu mixture and scallions. Bake in hot oven for 12 minutes. Cut into squares or triangles. Serve with a green salad as an appetizer or light meal.

Note: To toast nuts, heat them in a dry frying pan over medium heat until fragrant and golden. Shake the pan occasionally and watch carefully so nuts do not burn.

Makes 2 tarts; serves 4

Variations

Add black olives and/or capers to the tofu mixture.

Cut pastry sheet into 8 pieces to make 8 small tarts.

TOMATO AND TOFU TART WITH BASIL PESTO

Shredded beet strudel with yogurt-cucumber sauce

FOR YOGURT-CUCUMBER SAUCE

3¹/₂ oz (105 g) silken firm or silken soft tofu,
   pureed

¹/₂ cup (4 oz/125 g) plain (natural) yogurt

1 small English (hothouse) cucumber, seeded and
   diced

1 tablespoon fresh lemon juice

1 garlic clove, finely chopped

salt and cracked pepper to taste

1 cup (8 oz/250 g) grated carrot

1 cup (8 oz/250 g) grated beets (beetroots)

1 cup (8 oz/250 g) firm or extra-firm tofu,
   shredded

2 tablespoons finely chopped fresh parsley

pinch cayenne pepper

¹/₄ teaspoon grated fresh ginger

2 scallions (shallots/spring onions), finely
   chopped

8 sheets thawed frozen phyllo pastry

olive-oil cooking spray

2 teaspoons sesame seeds

To make yogurt-cucumber sauce: In a food processor, puree tofu and yogurt until smooth. Pour into a medium bowl and add all remaining ingredients, stirring well to combine. Set aside.

In a large bowl, combine carrot, beets, tofu, parsley, pepper, ginger and scallions. Keeping the remaining sheets covered with a damp cloth, lightly spray 2 sheets phyllo pastry with oil. Place one on top of the other and fold in half. Place a quarter of vegetable mixture in center of folded sheet. Fold one end and both sides over filling, then roll to enclose the filling. Repeat with remaining phyllo and filling. Spray rolls lightly with oil and sprinkle with sesame seeds. Place rolls on a prepared pan and bake in a moderately hot oven (400°F/200°C) until cooked and crisp, about 20 minutes. Serve with yogurt-cucumber sauce and a tossed salad.

Makes 4

Variation

Add chopped cilantro (fresh coriander) leaves to the yogurt-cucumber sauce.

SHREDDED BEET STRUDEL WITH YOGURT-CUCUMBER SAUCE 55

Thai green curry mushrooms with herbed coconut sauce

3¹/₂ oz (105 g) firm or extra-firm tofu, shredded

¹/₂ cup (1 oz/30 g) fresh soy and linseed bread crumbs (bread available from natural foods stores)

4 jumbo shrimp (king prawns), shelled and chopped

¹/₄ cup (¹/₃ oz/10 g) finely chopped fresh chives

1 garlic clove, finely chopped

2 tablespoons Thai green curry paste

4 medium portobello flat mushrooms, stemmed

vegetable-oil cooking spray

5 oz (150 g) tempeh

1 tablespoon ketjap manis

2 oz (60 g) baby spinach leaves or mixed salad greens

¹/₂ red bell pepper (capsicum), seeded and thinly sliced

2 scallions (shallots/spring onions), green parts only, diagonally sliced

Herbed coconut sauce (page 34)

Preheat oven to 400°F (200°C). Lightly grease a baking sheet or line it with parchment (baking) paper. In a large bowl, combine tofu, bread crumbs, shrimp, chives, garlic and curry paste. Spray mushrooms lightly with oil. Fill each mushroom with one-fourth tofu mixture. Place mushrooms on baking sheet and bake for 20 minutes.

While mushrooms are baking, cut tempeh in half lengthwise and slice horizontally into 4 thin slices. Brush both sides of slices with ketjap manis and bake until browned, 5–6 minutes.

Divide spinach and bell pepper among 4 plates. Arrange 2 tempeh slices on spinach and top with a mushroom and scallions. Serve with herbed coconut sauce.

Serves 4

THAI GREEN CURRY MUSHROOMS WITH COCONUT SAUCE

Herb and tofu chicken with fresh tomato sauce

FOR GARLIC MASHED POTATOES

2 lbs (1 kg) potatoes, peeled and diced

2 unpeeled cloves garlic

1/4 teaspoon salt

1/4 teaspoon pepper

3 1/2 oz (105 g) silken firm or silken soft
   tofu, drained

2 tablespoons olive oil

3 1/2 oz (105 g) firm tofu, drained

2 1/2 oz (75 g) soy cheese

1 small onion, finely diced

1/2 cup (2 oz/60 g) dried bread crumbs

1 egg

1 tablespoon finely chopped fresh parsley

1 tablespoon finely chopped fresh chives

1/2 cup (2 oz/60 g) ground toasted macadamia
   nuts

ground black pepper to taste

4 chicken breast fillets

1 tablespoon vegetable or sunflower oil

Fresh tomato sauce (page 72) for serving

To make mashed potatoes: In a dry frying pan over medium heat, toast garlic until evenly browned, about 12 minutes. Remove peel and mash. Cook potatoes in salted boiling water, or steam, until tender, 8–10 minutes. Drain and mash with garlic, salt, pepper, tofu and olive oil. Set aside and keep warm.

Preheat oven to 350°F (180°C).

Crumble tofu and cheese until they resemble coarse bread crumbs. In a large bowl, combine tofu, cheese, onion, bread crumbs, egg, parsley, chives, nuts and pepper. Cut a slit lengthwise along one side of each chicken breast, halfway through, to create a pocket. Fill each pocket with tofu mixture and seal opening with toothpicks.

In a large frying pan, heat oil over medium heat and cook chicken until lightly browned, 1–2 minutes on each side. Transfer chicken to a lightly greased baking pan and bake in a moderate oven (350°F/180°C) until opaque throughout, 12–15 minutes. To test if chicken is cooked, insert a skewer into the thickest part of chicken flesh. If juices are clear, not pink, chicken is cooked. Serve on mashed potatoes with fresh tomato sauce.

Serves 4

HERB AND TOFU CHICKEN WITH FRESH TOMATO SAUCE

Chili-peanut chicken with hokkien noodles

10 oz (300 g) firm tofu, drained

2 tablespoons peanut oil

10 oz (300 g) boneless chicken thighs, thinly sliced

1 medium onion, sliced

1 clove garlic, finely chopped

1 teaspoon grated fresh ginger

1/2 cup (4 oz/125 g) crunchy peanut butter

1/4 cup (2 fl oz/60 ml) sweet chili sauce

2/3 cup (5 fl oz/150 ml) coconut milk

3/4 cup (6 fl oz/180 ml) chicken stock

2 tablespoons fresh lime juice

1 small red bell pepper (capsicum), thinly sliced

13 oz (400 g) ready-made, vacuum-sealed hokkien noodles

1 tablespoon finely chopped cilantro (fresh coriander)

4 oz (125 g) snow peas (mange-tout), diagonally sliced

2 scallions (shallots/spring onions), green parts only, diagonally sliced

Cut tofu into 1/2-inch (12-mm) dice. In a wok or large frying pan, heat oil over medium heat and fry tofu until lightly browned, about 1 minute on each side. Remove from pan and keep warm. Add remaining oil and fry chicken until golden, 3–4 minutes. Remove from pan and keep warm. Sauté onion, garlic and ginger until onion is soft, 3–4 minutes. Add peanut butter, chili sauce, coconut milk, stock, lime juice, and bell pepper and stir to combine. Add tofu and chicken and simmer for 10 minutes, adding extra chicken stock if sauce becomes too thick.

Meanwhile, to prepare noodles: Rinse noodles in hot water and separate gently. Drain. Add to tofu mixture with cilantro and snow peas, tossing well to combine. Heat through and serve immediately, garnished with scallions.

Serves 4

Variations

Omit chicken and increase quantity of tofu for a vegetarian meal.

Substitute beef or seafood for chicken.

Scrambled tofu with ginger calamari

12 dried shiitake mushrooms

2 tablespoons vegetable or sunflower oil

6 oz (180 g) calamari rings

2 large carrots, julienned

1 tablespoon grated fresh ginger

15 oz (450 g) firm tofu, drained

1¹/₂ tablespoons mirin or sweet white wine

3 tablespoons Japanese soy sauce

1 teaspoon sugar (optional)

6 scallions (shallots/spring onions), cut into
³/₄-inch (2-cm) diagonal slices

Soak dried mushrooms in warm water to soften, about 20 minutes. Discard stems and thinly slice caps.

In a large frying pan or wok, heat oil over high heat and sauté calamari just until it changes color. Remove from pan and keep warm. Reduce heat to medium and sauté mushrooms, carrots and ginger for 3–4 minutes. Add drained tofu and mash gently into large pieces. Increase heat to medium-high and stir in mirin, soy sauce and sugar. Cook, stirring occasionally, until liquid is nearly absorbed, 3–4 minutes. (Do not stir too much or tofu will break up too finely.) Add calamari and scallions, reserving a few scallions for garnish. Cook for 2 minutes. Serve garnished with scallions.

Serves 3–4

Variation

Substitute chicken, beef, shrimp or Japanese fish sticks (chikuwa) *for the calamari.*

SCRAMBLED TOFU WITH GINGER CALAMARI

Grilled tuna and tempeh with tofu

FOR AVOCADO, LIME AND WASABI TOFU

4 oz (125 g) silken tofu, drained

2 teaspoons shiro (white) miso

4 teaspoons white vinegar

1 avocado, peeled, pitted and diced

salt and pepper to taste

1 1/2 tablespoons fresh lime juice

1 teaspoon wasabi paste

5 oz (150 g) tempeh

vegetable-oil cooking spray

1 tablespoon teriyaki sauce

4 tuna fillets, about 5 oz (150 g) each

2 limes, sliced or halved

2 scallions (shallots/spring onions), green parts

  only, finely sliced diagonally

To make avocado, lime and wasabi tofu: In a food processor, process tofu until smooth. In a cup, combine 2 tablespoons pureed tofu with miso and stir until smooth. Return to food processor, add remaining ingredients and process until well combined, about 20–30 seconds. Set aside.

Light a fire in a charcoal grill (or use an oiled grill pan over high heat). Cut tempeh in half vertically, then cut horizontally into slices 1/8 inch (3 mm) thick. Brush slices with teriyaki sauce. Grill tuna for 2–3 minutes on each side for medium rare (do not overcook or it will become tough). Transfer to a plate. Grill tempeh and lime slices until lightly browned, 1–2 minutes on each side of tempeh and about 2 minutes for limes. Serve tuna with tempeh and avocado, lime and wasabi tofu, garnished with scallions and lime slices.

Serves 4

Variations

Serve avocado, lime and wasabi tofu as a dip with crackers and crisp vegetable sticks.

Use avocado tofu as a sandwich or wrap filling or savory crepe filling.

GRILLED TUNA AND TEMPEH WITH TOFU

Grilled-vegetable timbales with lemon-spinach sauce

FOR PARSNIP CRISPS (OPTIONAL GARNISH)

1 small parsnip, cut into long, thin shreds

vegetable or sunflower oil for frying

FOR LEMON SPINACH SAUCE

4 cups (4 oz/125 g) baby spinach leaves

2 tablespoons fresh lemon juice

1 clove garlic, finely chopped

3 tablespoons light olive oil

5 oz (150 g) firm tofu, drained

1/3 cup (3 fl oz/90 ml) balsamic vinegar

1/4 cup (2 fl oz/60 ml) olive oil

1 red bell pepper (capsicum), seeded and
   quartered

3 baby Japanese long eggplants (aubergines),
   thinly sliced crosswise

2 medium zucchini, thinly sliced crosswise

1 small sweet potato, peeled and thinly sliced
   crosswise

To make parsnip crisps: In a small saucepan, heat 2 inches (5 cm) oil over medium heat to 365°F (185°C). Deep-fry or panfry parsnip shreds in batches until golden. Drain on paper towels.

To make lemon spinach sauce: In a food processor, combine spinach, lemon juice, garlic and oil and puree until smooth. Set aside.

Light a fire in a charcoal grill (or use an oiled grill pan over high heat). Cut tofu into slices 1/2 inch (12 mm) thick and marinate in 2 tablespoons of the balsamic vinegar for 15 minutes. Drain and pat dry with paper towels. In a bowl, combine olive oil and remaining vinegar. Brush vegetables with oil mixture. Grill tofu and vegetables until lightly browned, 2–3 minutes on each side for tofu and 3–4 minutes on each side for vegetables.

Lightly grease four 6-fl-oz (180-ml) ramekins and layer each with 1 eggplant, 1 tofu, 1 teaspoon spinach sauce, 1 sweet potato slice, 1 bell pepper slice, 1 zucchini slice and another sweet potato slice. To serve, invert each timbale onto a small plate, swirl extra spinach sauce around timbale and garnish with parsnip crisps.

Makes 4

GRILLED-VEGETABLE TIMBALES

Grilled tofu steaks with roasted pepper sauce

FOR ROASTED PEPPER SAUCE

2 red bell peppers (capsicums)

4 unpeeled cloves garlic

1 teaspoon salt

2 tablespoons olive oil

10 oz (300 g) firm tofu, drained

1/4 teaspoon Asian sesame oil

2 tablespoons teriyaki sauce

5 oz (150 g) sweet potato, peeled and thinly sliced

olive-oil cooking spray

2 oz (60 g) snow peas (mange-tout) or sugar
   snap, julienned

4 cups (4 oz/125 g) firmly packed baby spinach
   leaves

2 teaspoons olive oil

salt and pepper to taste

To make roasted pepper sauce: Place bell peppers and garlic on a baking sheet in a preheated 350°F (180°C) oven and bake until peppers have softened, 30–40 minutes. Place peppers in a plastic bag, close and let cool. Remove seeds and skin. In a food processor, puree peppers with peeled garlic, salt and olive oil until smooth.

Light a fire in a charcoal grill (or use an oiled grill pan over high heat).

Cut tofu into horizontal slices 1/2 inch (12 mm) thick. In a shallow bowl, combine sesame oil and teriyaki sauce and marinate tofu for 15 minutes. Drain tofu and grill until browned, about 1 minute on each side. Lightly spray sweet potato with cooking-oil spray and grill on medium heat until just cooked through, 2–3 minutes on each side. Blanch snow peas in boiling water for 2 minutes. Drain.

Divide spinach leaves among 4–6 plates and sprinkle with snow peas, olive oil, salt and pepper. Divide sweet potato slices and hot tofu slices among plates. Drizzle 2–3 tablespoons roasted pepper sauce over each serving of tofu and serve immediately.

Serves 4–6

Seared salmon with spinach noodles

4 salmon fillets, 5 oz (150 g) each, skin and pin
   bones removed

2 tablespoons teriyaki sauce

Lemon-tofu cream (page 94)

1 clove garlic, finely chopped

pinch salt

8 oz (250 g) Asian dried spinach noodles

1 tablespoon finely chopped fresh dill

1 tablespoon finely chopped fresh flat-leaf parsley

1 tablespoon light olive oil

2 scallions (shallots/spring onions), cut into
   $3/_4$-inch (2-cm) diagonal slices

Light a fire in a charcoal grill or use an oiled grill pan over medium-high heat.

Marinate salmon with teriyaki sauce and let stand for 15 minutes. In a small saucepan, combine tofu cream, garlic and salt. Heat gently over low heat. Set aside and keep warm.

In a large pot of salted water, cook noodles until tender, 5–8 minutes. Drain. Toss noodles with dill, parsley and oil. Set aside and keep warm.

Drain salmon. Grill until just barely transluscent in center, 2–3 minutes on each side.

Divide noodles among 4 bowls and top with tofu cream and salmon. Garnish with scallions and serve immediately.

Serves 4

Tip

Chinese dried wheat noodles made with spinach are

available from Asian markets and supermarkets.

SEARED SALMON WITH SPINACH NOODLES

Tempeh with egg noodles and fresh tomato sauce

FOR FRESH TOMATO SAUCE

1 lb (500 g) vine-ripened or plum (roma) tomatoes

2 tablespoons olive oil

1 small onion, diced

3 tablespoons tomato paste

2 teaspoons Worcestershire sauce

$1/2$ teaspoon sugar

$1/4$ teaspoon salt

2 tablespoons chopped fresh parsley

2 tablespoons chopped fresh basil

$1/4$ teaspoon cayenne or 1 small red chili pepper,
   seeded and chopped (optional)

2 tablespoons olive oil

8 oz (250 g) tempeh, sliced into $1/2$-inch (12-mm)
   fingers

$1/2$ cup ($2^1/2$ oz/75 g) black olives, pitted

12 oz (375 g) dried egg noodles or preferred pasta

$1/4$ cup ($1/3$ oz/10 g) finely chopped fresh parsley

$1/4$ cup (1 oz/30 g) grated Parmesan cheese

To make fresh tomato sauce: Cut a small cross in each tomato and place in boiling water for 30–40 seconds. Drain and rinse tomatoes under cold water. Peel off skin, remove seeds and coarsely chop. In medium saucepan, heat oil over medium heat and sauté onion until softened, 3–4 minutes. Reduce heat, add remaining ingredients and simmer until tomatoes are soft. Puree in a blender. Return to saucepan, set aside and keep warm.

In a large frying pan, heat oil over medium heat and fry tempeh until lightly browned, about 2 minutes on each side. Add tempeh and olives to tomato sauce and simmer while noodles are cooking. In a large pot of salted boiling water, cook noodles until tender, 8–10 minutes (see package directions if cooking other pasta). Drain and serve topped with tomato sauce, parsley and Parmesan.

Serves 4

Variations

Combine tomato sauce with pureed silken tofu and serve as a creamy tomato soup with tempeh crisps (see page 50).

Substitute $14^1/2$ oz (440 g) of canned tomatoes for fresh tomatoes.

Add capers to tomato sauce if desired.

Chicken and noodle parcels

4 strips kampyo (gourd) each 8 inches (20 cm)
  long

4 dried shiitake mushrooms

3 oz (90 g) dried rice noodles (rice sticks)

2 large or 4 small thin deep-fried tofu pouches
  (aburaage)

FOR SEASONING LIQUID

1/2 cup (4 fl oz/125 ml) dashi or chicken stock

1 tablespoon Japanese soy sauce

1 teaspoon mirin or sweet white wine

1 teaspoon sake

pinch salt

FOR BROTH

6 cups (48 fl oz/1.5 L) dashi or chicken stock

3 tablespoons Japanese soy sauce

2 tablespoons sake

2 tablespoons mirin

pinch salt

2 oz (60 g) ground (minced) chicken

1 small carrot, julienned

1/4 cup (2 oz/60 g) thinly sliced water chestnuts

mustard for serving (optional)

Garlic mashed potatoes (page 58), for serving
  (optional)

Rub kampyo with wetted salt for 1 minute. Soak kampyo and mushrooms separately in warm water until soft, 15–20 minutes. Drain. Discard mushroom stems and thinly slice tops. In a heatproof bowl, cover noodles with boiling water and soak until soft, 5–8 minutes. Cut large tofu pouches in half crosswise or split ends of small tofu pouches and open. Pour boiling water over tofu to remove excess oil. Drain, squeeze out excess water and pat dry. Drain noodles and rinse under hot water. Drain again and cut into 2-inch (5-cm) lengths.

In a medium saucepan, combine all seasoning liquid ingredients and bring to a boil. Add mushrooms, chicken, carrots and noodles and simmer until most of liquid is absorbed. Add water chestnuts and fill each tofu pouch about two thirds full with mixture. Tie top of each sack with a kampyo strip.

To make broth: In a large saucepan, combine all broth ingredients and bring to a boil. Reduce heat, add tofu pouches, cover, and simmer for 20 minutes. Serve with mustard and garlic mashed potatoes.

Serves 4

Tip

The green parts of small scallions (shallots/spring onions) or chives can be used instead of kampyo strips.

Moroccan chicken with almond couscous

2 oz (60 g) small deep-fried tofu puffs

2 tablespoons olive oil

12 oz (375 g) boneless chicken thighs, chopped

1 medium red (Spanish) onion, sliced

1 garlic clove, finely chopped

1 teaspoon ground coriander

1 teaspoon ground cumin

1/4 teaspoon ground turmeric

1/2 cup (3 oz/90 g) dried apricots, sliced

1/4 teaspoon ground cinnamon

4 cups (32 fl oz/1 L) chicken stock

14 1/2 oz (440 g) canned tomatoes

3 baby Japanese or 2 baby globe eggplants
   (aubergines), thickly sliced

1 cup (5 oz/150 g) diced butternut squash or
   pumpkin, peeled

3 oz (90 g) firm tofu, diced

1 small green bell pepper (capsicum), seeded
   and diced

FOR ALMOND COUSCOUS

2 cups (12 oz/375 g) instant couscous

1/2 cup (2 1/2 oz/75 g) green peas

2 cups (16 fl oz/500 ml) boiling water

1 tablespoon butter

pinch salt

1/4 cup (1 1/2 oz/45 g) dried currants

1/3 cup (2 oz/60 g) almonds, toasted (see tip)

Pour boiling water over tofu puffs to remove excess oil. Drain, let cool to touch and squeeze out excess water. In a large saucepan or frying pan, heat oil and sauté chicken over medium heat until lightly browned, 3–4 minutes. Remove from heat and set aside; keep warm. Sauté onion and garlic in same pan until onion is soft, 3–4 minutes. Add coriander, cumin and turmeric and cook for 2 minutes. In a large saucepan, combine chicken, apricots, cinnamon, stock, tomatoes, eggplants, squash, tofu puffs, diced tofu and bell pepper. Reduce heat and simmer until sauce has thickened and vegetables are tender, 25–30 minutes.

Meanwhile, make almond couscous: In a heatproof bowl, combine couscous and peas. Pour in boiling water and stir in butter, salt and currants. Cover and let stand until liquid is absorbed, about 10 minutes. Stir in nuts. Serve with Moroccan chicken.

Serves 4

Tip

To toast almonds: Toast almonds in a dry frying pan over medium heat, shaking pan occasionally to prevent nuts from burning.

MOROCCAN CHICKEN WITH ALMOND COUSCOUS

Pork and tofu on lemongrass skewers

FOR HERBED JASMINE RICE

1½ cups (10½ oz/330 g) jasmine rice

2½ cups (20 fl oz/625 ml) water

2 tablespoons finely chopped parsley

2 tablespoons finely chopped chives

5 oz (150 g) extra-firm tofu, drained

1 lb (500 g) ground (minced) pork

1 teaspoon grated fresh ginger

2 small red chili peppers, seeded

2 cloves garlic, minced

1 tablespoon soy sauce

1 teaspoon Chinese five-spice powder

2 scallions (shallots/spring onions), finely
  chopped

¼ teaspoon salt

4 stalks lemongrass, white part only, each cut into
  four 5-inch (13-cm) spears

2 tablespoons vegetable or sunflower oil

To make herbed jasmine rice: In a medium saucepan, combine rice and water, cover and bring to a boil. Reduce heat and simmer, covered, until water is absorbed, 12–15 minutes. Remove from heat and let stand, covered, for 10 minutes. Stir in parsley and chives. Set aside and keep warm.

Crumble tofu until it resembles coarse bread crumbs. In a large bowl, combine tofu, pork, ginger, chili peppers, garlic, soy sauce, five-spice powder, scallions and salt. Mix until well combined. Rinse hands in cold water, shaking off excess, and shape about ⅓ cup of tofu mixture around bottom half of each piece of lemongrass. In a large frying pan, heat oil over medium heat and cook skewers, turning occasionally, until meat is lightly browned, 6–8 minutes. Serve with minted jasmine rice.

Serves 4

Variations

Instead of frying, grill skewers on a grill or barbecue.

Form the pork and tofu mixture into small patties and use as a filling for tofu wraps (page 38).

Form mixture into bite-sized meatballs. Bake in a preheated 350°F (180°C) for 6–8 minutes. Serve each in a small lettuce cup with a dipping sauce as finger food.

PORK AND TOFU ON LEMONGRASS SKEWERS

Asparagus with creamy lemon and dill tofu

6 oz (180 g) firm tofu, drained

1 teaspoon grated lemon zest

2 1/2 tablespoons fresh lemon juice

1 teaspoon light soy sauce

1 clove garlic, finely chopped

generous pinch salt

2 tablespoons finely chopped fresh dill

2 bunches asparagus, trimmed

1/4 cup (1 oz/30 g) coarsely chopped macadamia
 nuts, toasted

cracked black pepper to taste

In a food processor, puree tofu until smooth. Add lemon zest and juice, soy sauce, garlic, salt and all but 1 teaspoon dill. Puree until smooth. Set aside.

Blanch asparagus in boiling water until crisp-tender, 2–3 minutes. Plunge into cold water to stop cooking process and set color. Drain. Serve asparagus with creamy lemon and dill tofu, sprinkled with macadamia nuts, the reserved dill and cracked pepper.

To toast macadamia nuts: Heat nuts in a dry frying pan over moderate heat until fragrant and golden, shaking pan occasionally so they do not burn.

Serves 4

Variations

Substitute mint for dill. Substitute or add other vegetables, such as broccoli, potatoes, beans or artichokes.

ASPARAGUS WITH CREAMY LEMON AND DILL TOFU

Leeks and green beans

1 large pouch deep-fried tofu (aburaage)

2 tablespoons olive oil

2 leeks (white part only), rinsed and chopped

1 garlic clove, finely chopped

10 oz (300 g) green beans, trimmed and halved
   crosswise

2 tablespoons light soy sauce

Pour boiling water over tofu to remove excess oil. Let cool to touch. Squeeze out excess water and slice tofu thinly. In a large frying pan, heat oil over medium heat and sauté leeks, garlic and tofu until leeks are tender but not browned, about 10 minutes. Add beans and sauté until crisp-tender, 2–3 minutes. Stir in soy sauce and serve.

Serves 4

Gingered sweet potatoes

1 lb (500 g) sweet potato, peeled and diced

8 oz (250 g) soft or silken firm or silken soft tofu

1 tablespoon packed brown sugar

1 teaspoon grated fresh ginger

1/2 teaspoon ground cinnamon

salt and pepper to taste

Preheat oven to 350°F (180°C). In a small saucepan of salted boiling water, or in a steamer, cook or steam potatoes until tender, 8–10 minutes. In a blender, combine potatoes and all remaining ingredients. Puree until smooth. Pour into greased baking dish and bake for 20 minutes.

Serves 4 as a side dish

Baby spinach, grapefruit and pine nut salad

5 cups (5 oz/150 g) baby spinach leaves

2 small grapefruit, peeled and segmented

4 oz (125 g) silken firm tofu, drained and cut into
  ³/₄-inch (2-cm) dice

3 tablespoons olive oil

2 tablespoons fresh lemon juice

1 tablespoon white wine vinegar

¹/₂ teaspoon salt

1 teaspoon sugar

cracked black pepper to taste

¹/₃ cup (1¹/₂ oz/45 g) roasted pine or
  macadamia nuts

FOR GARLIC FLAKES

3 garlic cloves, thinly sliced

¹/₃ cup (3 fl oz/90 ml) vegetable or sunflower oil

Divide spinach, grapefruit, and tofu among 4 salad plates. In a screw-top jar, combine oil, lemon juice, salt, sugar and pepper. Secure lid and shake well to combine and dissolve sugar. Pour over salad and garnish with pine nuts and garlic flakes. Serve as an accompaniment to fish or between courses to refresh the palate.

To make garlic flakes: In a small saucepan, heat oil over medium heat and cook garlic slices until golden, 30–60 seconds. Drain on paper towels.

Serves 4

Variation

Add cooked shrimp (prawns) and/or calamari

for a more substantial salad.

BABY SPINACH, GRAPEFRUIT AND PINE NUT SALAD

Smoked chicken and celery root salad

1 cup 3 oz (90 g) shredded celery root (celeriac)

1 cup 3 oz (90 g) shredded red cabbage

1 small red (Spanish) onion, shredded

1 small green apple, grated with skin on

1/3 cup (1 1/2 oz/45 g) coarsely chopped walnuts

2 tablespoons finely chopped fresh mint

13 oz (400 g) sliced smoked chicken

FOR MUSTARD SEED DRESSING

4 oz (125 g) soft or silken tofu, drained

1 1/2 tablespoons fresh lemon juice

2 1/2 tablespoons mustard seed oil or light olive oil

1/4 cup (2 oz/60 g) plain (natural) yogurt

1/2 teaspoon dry mustard

1/4 teaspoon cracked black pepper

In a large bowl, combine celery root, cabbage, onion and apple. Add walnuts and mint, reserving some of each for garnish. Pour dressing over salad and toss to combine. Serve with sliced chicken, garnished with reserved walnuts and mint.

To make mustard seed dressing: In food processor, puree tofu until smooth and creamy. Add remaining ingredients and process until well combined.

Serves 4

Variation

Substitute grilled or pan-fried fish fillets for chicken.

SMOKED CHICKEN AND CELERY ROOT SALAD

Strawberry ice cream

1 cup (8 fl oz/250 ml) water

1 cup (8 oz/250 g) sugar

10 oz (300 g) almond-flavored tofu, drained

2 cups (8 oz/250 g) strawberries, hulled

4–6 chocolate or waffle cups

fresh fruit for serving

grated dark chocolate for garnish

In a medium saucepan, combine water and sugar and bring to a boil, stirring until sugar has dissolved. Continue boiling gently for 7 minutes. Remove from heat and let cool to room temperature.

In a food processor, puree tofu until smooth. Add strawberries and puree until smooth. Gradually pour in the cooled syrup and process until combined. Pour mixture into an airtight container and freeze for 2 hours. Remove from freezer and whisk with a fork. Freeze 2 hours longer. Whisk again and return to freezer until fully frozen. Use a melon baller or small ice cream scoop to shape balls of ice cream and serve in chocolate or waffle cups with fresh fruit and grated chocolate.

Serves 4–6

Tip

Chocolate and waffle cups are available at most supermarkets.

STRAWBERRY ICE CREAM

Tofu pears with lime marmalade sauce

4 blocks (2 oz/60 g total) freeze-dried tofu, reconstituted (see page 23)

³/₄ cup (6 fl oz/180 ml) water

¹/₃ cup (3 oz/90 g) lime marmalade

3 tablespoons light soy sauce

¹/₄ cup (1¹/₂ oz/50g) all-purpose (plain) flour

2 eggs, lightly beaten with 2 tablespoons water

¹/₄ cup (2 oz/60 g) shredded or flaked wheat cereal, crushed

2 tablespoons shredded coconut

vegetable or sunflower oil for frying

1 firm unpeeled pear, halved and cored

juice of 1 lemon

Gently squeeze most of liquid from freeze-dried tofu. In a medium saucepan, combine tofu, water, marmalade, and soy sauce. Gradually bring to a boil, reduce heat and simmer for 15 minutes, turning tofu occasionally. Remove from heat and let cool for about 5 minutes.

Drain and squeeze excess moisture from tofu, reserving cooking liquid. Cut each tofu block in half horizontally. Cut each slice in half crosswise and then cut each piece in half diagonally to make a total of 8 triangles.

Put flower and egg mixture in separate shallow bowls. In another shallow bowl, mix crushed wheat biscuits and coconut. Lightly dust triangles with flour and dip into egg mixture, draining off any excess. Roll in crushed wheat mixture.

Fill a large frying pan or wok one-third full with oil and heat to 365°F (185°C). Deep-fry tofu triangles in batches until golden, 2–3 minutes. Drain on paper towels. Thinly slice pear and sprinkle slices with lemon juice to prevent browning. Arrange one-fourth of pear slices on each plate and top with tofu. Serve immediately with individual bowls of reserved tofu cooking liquid.

Serves 4

Baked coconut and tofu custard

FOR CUSTARD

10 oz (300 g) coconut-flavored tofu, drained

1 large egg

1½ tablespoons maple syrup or honey

2 teaspoons vanilla extract (essence)

½ cup (4 fl oz/125 ml) heavy (double) cream

FOR BLUEBERRY SAUCE

2 cups (8 oz/250 g) blueberries

2 tablespoons sugar

Preheat oven to 350°F (180°C). In a food processor, combine all custard ingredients and puree until smooth. Pour mixture into six 4-fl-oz (125-ml) cups or ramekins. Place cups in a baking dish and fill baking dish with water to come halfway up sides of cups. Cover baking dish with aluminum foil and bake until custard is set, 30–40 minutes.

Meanwhile, make blueberry sauce: In a small saucepan, combine berries and sugar and cook over medium heat, stirring occasionally, for 5 minutes. Remove from heat and strain mixture, pressing all liquid from berries with back of a large spoon. Let cool.

Serve custard hot or well chilled with blueberry sauce. If serving chilled, place cups of custard over bowls of ice for an impressive presentation and to keep custard cold. (Custard can become watery at room temperature.)

Serves 6

BAKED COCONUT AND TOFU CUSTARD

Tofu crepes with lemon-tofu cream

FOR LEMON-TOFU CREAM

6 oz (180 g) firm fresh tofu, drained

1 teaspoon grated lemon zest

2¹/₂ tablespoons fresh lemon juice

1 teaspoon light soy sauce

pinch salt

¹/₄ teaspoon ground cinnamon mixed with
   2 tablespoons white sugar

FOR CREPES

4 oz (125 g) silken tofu, drained

2 cups (16 fl oz/500 ml) soy milk

¹/₂ cup (4 fl oz/125 ml) water

¹/₂ teaspoon salt

2 cups (10 oz/300 g) self-rising flour, sifted

vegetable-oil cooking spray

fresh fruit for serving

To make lemon-tofu cream: In food processor, puree tofu until smooth. Add lemon zest, lemon juice, soy sauce and salt, and process until well combined. Set aside. In a small bowl, combine cinnamon and sugar. Set aside.

To make crepes: In a food processor, puree tofu until smooth. Add milk, water and salt and puree until well combined. Gradually stir in flour until smooth.

Heat a 9-inch (23-cm) crepe pan or frying pan over medium heat. Lightly spray with oil and pour in crepe batter, tilting pan to coat the bottom evenly. Cook until lightly browned, about 1 minute on each side. Transfer crepe to a heatproof plate and place in a slow oven (250°F/120°C) to keep warm. Repeat with remaining batter and crepes.

Fold 4 or 5 crepes on a serving plate, top with lemon-tofu cream and sprinkle with cinnamon sugar. Serve with fresh fruit.

Makes 20 crepes; serves 4–6

Tips

Crepes can be made ahead, stacked with a sheet of freezer plastic between each one and frozen in an airtight container or freezer bag for up to 1 month.

The crepes can be used with either sweet or savory fillings.

TOFU CREPES WITH LEMON-TOFU CREAM

Fresh fruit in chocolate pastry cups with lemon-tofu cream

FOR PASTRY

³/₄ cup (4 oz/125 g) all-purpose (plain) flour

4 tablespoons (2 oz/60 g) butter

1 tablespoon cold water

vegetable-oil cooking spray

FOR FILLING

1¹/₂ oz (45 g) dark chocolate, chopped

¹/₂ cup (2 oz/60 g) strawberries, hulled and sliced

2 kiwifruit, peeled and sliced

³/₄ cup lemon tofu cream (page 94)

grated dark chocolate for garnish

To make pastry: In a food processor, combine flour and butter and puree until mixture resembles bread crumbs. Add water and process for 30 seconds to combine. Transfer dough to a lightly floured surface and knead until well combined. Cover with plastic wrap and refrigerate for 30 minutes.

Preheat oven to 400°F (200°C). On a floured surface, roll pastry out to around ¹/₈ inch (3 mm) thick. Cut pastry into 3-inch (7.5-cm) squares or rounds and press pieces into lightly greased muffin cups or individual tart molds. Allowing excess pastry to protrude beyond the molds will give tarts a rustic look. Fit a square of parchment (baking) paper into each mold and fill with pie weights or dried beans to bake blind. Bake until golden, 10–15 minutes. Let cool.

To make filling: In a double boiler over barely simmering water, or microwave, melt chocolate. Spread about 1 teaspoon melted chocolate in base of each pastry shell and let set. Arrange sliced fruit in each cup and top with 2–3 teaspoons lemon-tofu cream. Sprinkle grated chocolate over.

Makes 10 tarts

Variations

Use other combinations of fruits, such as cantaloupe (rockmelon), mango, pears, blueberries or peaches.

Dice fruit and fold into lemon-tofu cream.

Make one 9-inch (23-cm) tart instead of individual pastries.

FRESH FRUIT IN CHOCOLATE PASTRY CUPS

Chocolate-banana pie

FOR PIE CRUST

17 wheatmeal biscuits, crushed

1 tablespoon sugar

3 teaspoons ground cinnamon

8 tablespoons (4 oz/125 g) butter, melted

FOR FILLING

1/4 cup (2 fl oz/60 ml) water

1/3 oz (10 g) plain gelatin or 3 teaspoons powder

3 1/2 oz (105 g) chocolate, coarsely chopped

1 teaspoon sugar

13 oz (400 g) silken firm tofu, drained

1/2 cup (4 fl oz/125 ml) heavy (double) cream

2 small bananas, sliced

1 teaspoon honey

banana slices for garnish

1 oz (30 g) dark chocolate

To make pie crust: In a medium bowl, combine crushed crackers, sugar and cinnamon. Stir in melted butter and press into a 9-inch (23-cm) round springform pan. Refrigerate.

To make filling: Put water in a small saucepan, sprinkle with gelatin and let stand for 1 minute. Add chocolate and sugar to saucepan and heat over medium heat, stirring constantly, until chocolate is melted. Do not boil. Remove from heat and let cool for 5 minutes.

In a food processor, puree tofu until smooth. Remove and reserve 1/3 cup (3 fl oz/90 ml) for decorating. With machine running, gradually add chocolate to remaining tofu and puree until well combined. Pour mixture into a large bowl.

In a deep bowl, beat cream until soft peaks form. Gently fold in whipped cream into tofu mixture. Line bottom and sides of pie crust with sliced bananas and pour in tofu mixture. Refrigerate until set, about 2 hours.

To serve, garnish top of pie with banana slices. In a small bowl, stir reserved tofu and honey together. Put in a pastry bag with large star nozzle and pipe decoration in center or around edge of pie top. Using a vegetable peeler, cut curls from block of chocolate and garnish pie.

Makes one 9-inch (23-cm) pie.

CHOCOLATE-BANANA PIE

Lime and almond tofu cheesecake

FOR PIE CRUST

14 wheatmeal biscuits

1 teaspoon ground cinnamon

7 tablespoons (3½ oz/100 g) butter, melted

FOR FILLING

1 lb 6 oz (680 g) soft tofu, well drained

3 eggs

⅓ cup (3 fl oz/90 ml) honey

2 teaspoons grated lime zest

¼ cup (2 fl oz/60 ml) fresh lime juice

½ cup (4½ oz/140 g) slivered almonds

2 tablespoons flaked or shredded coconut

Maple syrup cream (page 103) for serving
(optional)

To make pie crust: In a medium bowl, combine crushed crackers and cinnamon. Stir in melted butter and press into bottom of a 9-inch (23-cm) round springform pan. Refrigerate.

Preheat oven to 350°F (180°C).

To make filling: In a food processor, puree tofu, then add eggs, honey, lime zest and lime juice. Process until smooth. Pour into pie crust and decorate with almonds and coconut. Bake until a skewer inserted in center comes out clean, about 40 minutes. Let cool in pan. Serve with maple syrup cream.

Makes one 9-inch (23-cm) cake

Mango soufflé

12 oz (375 g) firm silken tofu, drained

2 cups (10 oz/300 g) chopped fresh or drained canned mango

2 teaspoons plain gelatin

3 tablespoons fresh lime juice

1 teaspoon honey

2 egg whites

1 tablespoon grated lime zest

In a food processor, puree tofu and mango until smooth. In a small bowl, combine gelatin over lime juice. Place bowl over hot water and stir until gelatin dissolves completely. Gradually stir gelatin and honey into tofu mixture.

In a large bowl, beat egg whites until soft peaks form. Gently fold egg whites through the tofu mixture, then spoon mixture into eight 4-fl-oz (125-ml) ramekins or cups and refrigerate until set. Garnish with lime zest to serve.

Makes 8 individual soufflés

Chili jam peaches with maple syrup cream

6 oz (180 g) firm tofu, drained

2 large unpeeled peaches, halved and pitted

1 tablespoon butter

3 tablespoons packed brown sugar

1 tablespoon mild chili jam

FOR MAPLE SYRUP CREAM

6 1/2 oz (200 g) silken tofu, drained

2 tablespoons maple syrup or honey

1 teaspoon vanilla extract (essence)

1 tablespoon fresh lemon juice

Cut tofu into slices 1/2 inch (12 mm) thick and pat dry with paper towel. Cut a small slice off from bottom of each peach half to make it stable or thickly slice. In a medium frying pan, combine butter and brown sugar. Stir over medium-low heat. Add peaches and cook 2–3 minutes, turning occasionally and being careful sugar does not burn.

Add chili jam and sliced tofu and cook until sugar is caramelized and peaches and tofu are well coated, 2–3 minutes. Serve each peach half topped with 3 or 4 tofu slices and maple syrup cream.

To make maple syrup cream: In a food processor, combine all ingredients for maple syrup cream and puree until smooth.

Serves 4

Variations

Substitute other fruit, such as pears, mango, fresh figs or pineapple, for peaches.

Slice peaches before cooking and serve in Tofu crepes (page 94).

Black sticky rice with lime

1 cup (7 oz/220 g) black sticky (glutinous) rice

2½ cups (20 fl oz/625 ml) water plus

  ¼ cup (2 fl oz/60 ml) water

1 cup (8 fl oz/250 ml) coconut milk

1 tablespoon packed palm sugar

  or dark brown sugar

1 teaspoon soy sauce

6 seasoned tofu pouches

6 unpeeled rambutan, halved, unpeeled or lychees

1 star fruit, sliced

¼ cup (2 fl oz/60 ml) fresh lime juice

Put rice in a medium bowl and add water to cover. Soak overnight; drain rice.

In a small saucepan, bring 2½ cups water to a boil and stir in rice. Return to a boil, reduce heat and simmer, uncovered, for 15 minutes. Drain.

In a medium saucepan, combine rice, coconut milk, palm sugar, soy sauce and ¼ cup (2 fl oz/60 ml) water and cook over medium-low heat, stirring constantly, until rice is thick and most of liquid is absorbed, 20–25 minutes. Let cool slightly. Open tofu pockets with fingers, pushing down to open each corner. Fill pockets two-thirds full with rice mixture. Fold sides of pouches over filling to form parcels and turn over so folded sides are on the bottom. Cut diagonally across parcels and arrange them on a plate with rambutans and star fruit. Sprinkle with lime juice, or serve lime juice separately to be added according to individual taste.

Serves 4–6

Tip

Rambutan and lychees are available from Asian markets. Substitute canned lychees if fresh are not available. Drain canned lychees before using.

Glossary

Bonito flakes: Flakes shaved from a dried piece of bonito fish. Coarse flakes are the basis of dashi, the traditional Japanese fish stock, and miso soup. Fine flakes are used as a garnish. Both are available in cellophane packets from Asian food stores.

Celeriac: Knobby root vegetable that tastes like celery and parsley. Peel and soak in water with a dash of lemon or vinegar to prevent discoloration before using raw in salads, or cook as a vegetable or add to stir-fries.

Chili jam: A sweet and spicy condiment with chilies, ranging from hot to quite mild.

Chili peppers: As a general rule, the smaller the chili the hotter it is. For a milder taste, remove seeds and membrane. Dried chili flakes and powder can be substituted.

Chinese five spice: Made from an equal mixture of ground Szechuan peppercorns, star anise, fennel, cloves and cinnamon. Available at most supermarkets.

Cilantro: Also known as coriander or Chinese parsley; always sold with its roots attached. The roots and stems are used in Thai green curry, the leaves have a pungent flavor and aroma and are popular as a garnish or flavoring in Asian and Mediterranean dishes.

Coconut milk and cream: Coconut milk is a rich liquid extracted from grated coconut flesh steeped in water. Thicker coconut cream adds more flavor than the thinner coconut milk. Popular in sweet and savory Asian dishes, both are available in cans from supermarkets.

Daikon: Also known as Japanese radish or long white carrot. Crisp, juicy and slightly sweet, this root vegetable should be peeled before shredding to use as a garnish or in salads, or stir-fried, baked or steamed. Also available pickled and used in sushi.

Dashi: Japanese fish stock made from dried bonito fish flakes (katsuobushi) and konbu/kombu (seaweed). Available in concentrated liquid, powder or dried granules from Asian food stores. Combine with water to required consistency. Dashi may be substituted with other stocks.

Gelatin: An odorless, tasteless and colorless setting agent. Available as a powder or thin sheets, which can vary in strength so check manufacturer's instructions. Mix powder with water and heat, without boiling, until dissolved before use.

Ghee: Unsalted butter that has been melted and the milk solids removed (clarified). It is then able to be heated to a high temperature without burning and develops a nutty flavor and aroma. Popular in Middle Eastern and Indian cooking. Available from supermarkets.

Ginger: Gnarled and bumpy root with a spicy, pungent odor and slightly sweet and peppery taste. Peel the paper-thin skin with the back of a knife before grating or chopping finely. Popular in Asian and Indian cooking.

Glutinous rice: Also known as sticky rice. Available as white grains or black if the bran coating is left on. Used for Asian desserts and sweets, and often combined with coconut milk.

Kampyo: Long, cream strips of gourd that are dried. Before using, rub with wetted salt for 1 minute then soften in water. Use as an edible tie for food parcels. Also sold seasoned in sweetened soy sauce and used in sushi. Dried strips are available in cellophane packs and seasoned strips in refrigerated packs from Asian food stores.

Ketjap manis: Also known as kecap manis. A thick, dark brown, syrupy sweet soy sauce from Indonesia. Sweetened with palm sugar and often seasoned with garlic and star anise, it is used as a marinade, dipping sauce or as a flavoring in stir-fries and other dishes. Available from supermarkets and Asian food stores.

Lemongrass: A popular lemon-scented grass in Asian-style dishes. Trim the root, discard top third and any tough outer layers, chopping finely or bruise (hitting with a meat mallet or blunt side of a chef's knife) to infuse flavor.

Mirin: Sweet Japanese rice wine available from Asian food stores and some supermarkets. Substitute with sweet sherry.

Noodles: Hokkien noodles are fresh yellow egg noodles. Rinse under warm water for a few minutes to separate noodles before use. Available in refrigerated vacuum-sealed packs from supermarkets. Shiratake noodles are thin, translucent, jelly-like noodles made from starch of the root vegetable, devil's tongue. With a neutral taste, the noodles will absorb flavors of the dish they are added to. Available dried or in brine in refrigerated packs from Asian food stores, which should be rinsed under hot water before use. Can substitute with harusame or vermicelli noodles.

Palm sugar: Made from the sap of the palm tree, the darker the color the more caramel the flavor. Available in wrapped blocks or jars from Asian food stores and some supermarkets. Thinly shave with a sharp knife or grate before use. Brown sugar can be substituted.

Plum sauce: This thick, sweet and slightly sour sauce is used as a flavoring, a dipping sauce or added to stir-fries. Available from supermarkets.

Rambutan: Also known as hairy lychee. Remove the spiky red coating to reveal the firm, smooth, white-fleshed fruit that tastes like grapes. Add to savory or fruit salads, Asian dishes or serve with cheese.

Shiitake mushrooms: Often called golden oak and Chinese black mushrooms. Available fresh and dried from supermarkets and Asian food stores. Soak dried mushrooms in warm water for 20 minutes to soften, discarding hard stems before use.

Soy sauce: Dark, salty sauce made from fermented soybeans and usually wheat. The best flavor is from naturally brewed sauces. Used to enhance the flavor of dishes and as a dipping sauce. Reduced-salt soy sauce is also available.

Sweet chili sauce: Mild and sweet, often flavored with garlic and/or ginger. Used as a flavoring or dipping sauce, often combined with plum, hoisin, ketjap manis or soy sauce.

Tabasco sauce: A spicy, hot sauce made from the tabasco chili so use sparingly to add zest to dishes. Seasoned and milder sauces are also available from supermarkets. It can be substituted with red pepper sauce.

Tahini: Smooth paste made from ground sesame seeds. Some are thicker than others, so add extra water if required. Available from most supermarkets.

Teriyaki sauce: Soy sauce seasoned with garlic, ginger, rice wine and vinegar. Used as a flavoring, marinade and dipping sauce. Available from supermarkets.

Thai red and green curry paste: Green curry paste is fragrant and spicy hot. Thai red curry paste can be substituted and although hot, is not usually as hot as green.

Turmeric: This bright orange, pungent and slightly bitter root is used to flavor and color dishes, especially Indian curries and rice. Sometimes available fresh, which should be peeled and finely grated before use.

Wasabi: Hot, Japanese green horseradish, traditionally served with sushi and sashimi. Available ready-to-use in tubes or powder that is mixed with water as required as pungency is easily lost. Occasionally available fresh; peel and finely grate in a circular motion.

Index

Guide to weights and measures

The conversions given in the recipes in this book are approximate. Whichever system you use, remember to follow it consistently, thereby ensuring that the proportions are consistent throughout a recipe.

WEIGHTS

Imperial	Metric
⅓ oz	10 g
½ oz	15 g
¾ oz	20 g
1 oz	30 g
2 oz	60 g
3 oz	90 g
4 oz (¼ lb)	125 g
5 oz (⅓ lb)	150 g
6 oz	180 g
7 oz	220 g
8 oz (½ lb)	250 g
9 oz	280 g
10 oz	300 g
11 oz	330 g
12 oz (¾ lb)	375 g
16 oz (1 lb)	500 g
2 lb	1 kg
3 lb	1.5 kg
4 lb	2 kg

VOLUME

Imperial	Metric	Cup
1 fl oz	30 ml	
2 fl oz	60 ml	¼
3 fl oz	90 ml	⅓
4 fl oz	125 ml	½
5 fl oz	150 ml	⅔
6 fl oz	180 ml	¾
8 fl oz	250 ml	1
10 fl oz	300 ml	1¼
12 fl oz	375 ml	1½
13 fl oz	400 ml	1⅔
14 fl oz	440 ml	1¾
16 fl oz	500 ml	2
24 fl oz	750 ml	3
32 fl oz	1L	4

USEFUL CONVERSIONS

¼ teaspoon	1.25 ml
½ teaspoon	2.5 ml
1 teaspoon	5 ml
1 Australian tablespoon	20 ml (4 teaspoons)
1 UK/US tablespoon	15 ml (3 teaspoons)

Butter/Shortening

1 tablespoon	½ oz	15 g
1½ tablespoons	¾ oz	20 g
2 tablespoons	1 oz	30 g
3 tablespoons	1 ½ oz	45 g

OVEN TEMPERATURE GUIDE

The Celsius (°C) and Fahrenheit (°F) temperatures in this chart apply to most electric ovens. Decrease by 25°F or 10°C for a gas oven or refer to the manufacturer's temperature guide. For temperatures below 325°F (160°C), do not decrease the given temperature.

Oven description	°C	°F	Gas Mark
Cool	110	225	¼
	130	250	½
Very slow	140	275	1
	150	300	2
Slow	170	325	3
Moderate	180	350	4
	190	375	5
Moderately Hot	200	400	6
Fairly Hot	220	425	7
Hot	230	450	8
Very Hot	240	475	9
Extremely Hot	250	500	10

First published in the United States in 2002 by Periplus Editions (HK) Ltd.,
with editorial offices at 153 Milk Street, Boston, Massachusetts 02109 and
130 Joo Seng Road #06-01/03
Olivine Building, Singapore 368357

Library of Congress Cataloging-in-Publication Data is available.
ISBN 0-7946-5007-4

DISTRIBUTED BY

North America
Tuttle Publishing
Distribution Center
Airport Industrial Park
364 Innovation Drive
North Clarendon, VT 05759-9436
Tel: (802) 773-8930
Tel: (800) 526-2778

Japan and Korea
Tuttle Publishing
RK Building, 2nd Floor
2-13-10 Shimo-Meguro, Meguro-Ku
Tokyo 153 0064
Tel: (03) 5437-0171
Fax: (03) 5437-0755

Asia Pacific
Berkeley Books Pte. Ltd.
130 Joo Seng Road
#06-01/03
Olivine Building
Singapore 368357
Tel: (65) 280-3320
Fax: (65) 280-6290

Set in Frutiger on QuarkXPress
Printed in Singapore

First Edition
07 06 05 04 03 02 10 9 8 7 6 5 4 3 2 1